21
DAYS TO
TRAIN YOUR DOG

21
DAYS TO
TRAIN
YOUR
DOG

COLIN TENNANT

FIREFLY BOOKS

21 DAYS TO TRAIN YOUR DOG

This book sets out to instruct you how to train a dog in a 21-day program. It gives advice on various training exercises and psychological programs to solve many training problems that owners often experience. The programs and training techniques described are quite safe but readers must be aware that dogs do vary in temperament, breed type and malleability, and it is incumbent upon the owner to select the training techniques they wish to apply to their dog bearing in mind its character, history and individual traits.

The information and recommendations in this book are given without any guarantees on behalf of the author and publisher, who disclaim any liability with the use of this material and the equipment described.

Published in the United States by
Firefly Books (U.S.) Inc.
P.O. Box 1338, Ellicott Station
Buffalo, New York 14205

Published in Canada by
Firefly Books Ltd.
66 Leek Crescent
Richmond Hill, Ontario L4B 1H1

Design: Philip Clucas
MSIAD

Printed in China

A FIREFLY BOOK

Published by Firefly Books Ltd. 2006

First printing

Publisher Cataloging-in-Publication Data (U.S.)
Tennant, Colin.
    21 days to train your dog / Colin Tennant.—1st ed.
    [160] p. : col. photos. ;   cm.
    Includes index.
    Summary: Annotated sequence photographs, computer graphics and text explain step-by-step dog training methods, advice on puppy training, equipment and effective ways of controlling demanding dogs.
    ISBN-13: 978-1-55407-012-1
    ISBN-10: 1-55407-012-0
    ISBN-13: 978-1-55407-133-3 (pbk.)
    ISBN-10: 1-55407-133-X (pbk.)
    1. Dogs — Training. I. Title.
    636.7 21   SF431.T46   2004

Library and Archives Canada
Cataloguing in Publication
Tennant, Colin
    21 days to train your dog / Colin Tennant. — 1st pbk. ed.
    Includes index.
    ISBN-13: 978-1-55407-133-3
    ISBN-10: 1-55407-133-X
    1. Dogs—Training. I. Title. II. Title:
    21 days to train your dog.
    SF431.T45 2006   636.7'0887
    C2005-906734-9

Contents

Chapter One: **Introduction** pages **8–13**
At Man's Side… A Marriage Made in Heaven… Training Styles… Why Are Some Dogs
Difficult to Train?… The Dog and its Innate Drives… Some Common Training Problems…
Come Here… The Pulling Battle… Jumping Jack and Other Attention Seekers

Chapter Two: **What Is Dog Training?** pages **14–19**
The Behavioral Aspect of Training… The Well-Mannered Dog…
The Challenges Awaiting You… Training Techniques… What Is a
Trained Dog?… Do We Need to Train Dogs?… Dogs and Children

Chapter Three: **The Leadership Program** pages **20–29**
The Wolf in Your House… How Does this Affect Training?… The House Plan… The
Bedroom… The Living Room… Easy Chairs… Out of My Way… Doors and Gates…
Feeding Your Dog… Tidbits, Treats and Food… Toys and Balls… Petting and Stroking…
The Ignore… Dog Training and the Leadership Program… Length of the Program… The
Hook – A Restriction Program for the Dominant Dog

Chapter Four:
Puppy Obedience Training pages **30–35**
One or Two Puppies?… Personality…
The Mind of a Pup… Puppy Training Plan…
Introduction of the Leash and Collar…
Sit and Down Stays

Chapter Five: **Training Equipment** pages **36–43**
Dog Body Harnesses… Dog Walking Harnesses…
Flexible Leash Training… Long Lines… Face
Collars… Introducing the Face Collar… Chain
Collars… Electronic Spray Collars…
Food, Toys and Other Playthings…
Deterrent Sprays… Dog Beds…
Training Discs… Whistles… Food
Rewards… A Clean Diet

21 DAYS TO TRAIN YOUR DOG

Chapter Six: **Communication** pages **44–53**

Creating a New Language… Inherited Behavior… Tone of Voice… Rewards… Unrewarding Experiences… Timing… Motivation and Consistency… Guilty or Not?… The Ignore — A Powerful Dominant Statement… Hand Signals… Sit… Stand… Down… Stay… Come (Recall)

Chapter Seven: **The 21-Day Training Plan** pages **54–59**

Commands Used… Training Program… Exercise Summary… Heel… Sit… Stand… Down… Stay… Recall… Free… Advice Before You Start

Chapter Eight: **Heelwork** pages **60–83**

Commands — A New Language… Heel Training for Puppies… Heel Turns… Heel — Walking Forward… The Left Turn… Making Turns with a Smaller Dog… The Left About Turn… The Right Turn… The Right About Turn… Heel Training with Dogs… Pay Attention… House Training Plan… Backyard Training Plan… Street Heelwork… Dog/Car Training… At the Park — Letting the Dog Out… Walking with a Stroller… Using Face Collars… Body Harnesses… The High Check Collar

Chapter Nine: **The Stay Positions** pages **84–123**

The Sit, Stand, Down and Stay Positions… The Sit Position… The Sit Using Food… The Sit Using Toys… The Ignore and Sit… The Sit Using a Hook… The Sit: Forward and Backward… The Sit: Leash and Collar Style… Sit/Stay — Introducing Hand Signals… Stay and Circle on the Leash… Sit/Stay — Time and Distance Training… The Stand Position… The Stand Using Turn and Food… The Stand Using Collar and Leash… The Stand Using Toys… The Stand, Touch and Tickle… The Stand Using a Hook… Stand/Stay… The Stand Position — Problem Solving… The Down Position… The Down Using Food… The Down Using a Toy… The Down Using a Collar and Leash… The Down Using a Hook… The

CONTENTS

Down Using a Push… Down/
Stay… Location Training… Sit/
Stand/Down/Stay Training — Week
2… Entering the Real World…
Training in Action — The Walk to
the Park… At the Park — Find
Your Training Area… The
Sit/Stay — Signal and Time…
Common Sit/Stay Problems… Stay Positions — Time and Distance Training… How Long
Should I Maintain Stay Positions?… Training Tips… The Stays — Week 3… Common Problems in the Park
or Street… Fun and Games… Going Home

Chapter Ten: The Recall pages **124–151**
Why Won't My Dog Come?… The Disinterested Owner… Delayed
Training… The Dog's Natural Drives… Puppy Recall… Recall
with a Toy… Problem Solving… Leash and Collar
Recall… Sound and Food Recall… The
Long-Line Recall… Yard Recall…
Training in the Park… Problem
Solving… Using Flexi-Leashes…
Whistle Recall… Hide and Seek
Recall… Electronic Spray
Collars

**Chapter Eleven: Keeping
It Going** pages **152–153**
Combining Training with a
Walk… Should I Join
a Training Club?

Chapter Twelve: Troubleshooting pages **154–155**
A Helping Hand… What If I Own Two Dogs?

Index pages **156–159**

Acknowledgments page **160**

CHAPTER ONE

Introduction

At Man's Side

Dogs are such a familiar part of our world that most people simply take them for granted and forget about the extraordinary bond that exists between dog and owner, a bond that has made us want to domesticate and share our homes with this unique creature for as long as we can remember.

Picture the scene — owner and dog may be playing a game on the living room floor. Upon hearing the doorbell, owner and dog sit up alertly — both want to investigate who might be at the door. If the visitor is invited inside, while the owner is busy being a good host, the dog is often excited and keen to meet the guest. Both dog and owner greet a known visitor very differently from a casual one, and this in itself demonstrates how this animal not only fits into the human family pack, but takes such an active part in the lifestyle of the family.

What other domesticated animal behaves in this way? What other animal takes such an interest in us and to such a great degree? What other animal responds to our physical and vocal language, and our mood changes with such sensitivity and understanding? None. The dog is King in fitting snugly into our lives no matter what circumstances we may live in. Whether you are rich or live a very humble existence, a dog accepts who you are and makes the best of it. Of course, like recalcitrant children in even the most close-knit of families, sometimes dogs will disobey, and this is the reason for *21 Days to Train Your Dog*.

A Marriage Made in Heaven

Dogs provide much for so many people in modern society. I feel that it is important that an owner understands a bit about their dog's mind and appreciates how it perceives and functions in our world. The fact that we can communicate as much as we do with dogs is probably the main reason that the wolf was invited into our homes in the first place.

What human have you met who is always welcoming when you arrive home, is never critical of you or your behavior, is always willing to be in your company whatever your mood, does not hold a grudge and can be so attentive so often? In truth, the virtues we look for in other people appear to be more reliably available in dogs. That may be the secret of their success in being accepted into the human fold.

Dogs don't try to put you down. Dogs are reliable, consistent and display excellent guarding skills, even if it is just an alert bark when someone approaches the home. Dogs are tactile creatures and this is also a powerful attraction — people get so much pleasure from stroking and playing with a dog. And, like raising a child, watch-

ing it grow, develop and learn new ideas, dogs seem to invoke the inner parent in us all and bring our nurturing instincts into play.

Unlike most humans, dogs appear instinctively prepared to stay by our sides whatever happens in our complicated lives. It goes without saying our brains are so big and complex that dogs cannot possibly understand the world as we do, but they certainly manage very well to fit into our lives right beside us.

Dogs have characteristics that flatter and appeal to us and this is another crucial factor in why we develop such close relationships with them. Of course dogs themselves also have instinctive drives that they follow, and so an element of conflict is inevitable in the canine-human relationship.

Though we share sufficient in common to live together amicably, just as in human relationships, domestic disputes do arise and need to be addressed. This is why understanding and training your dog is so important.

Training Styles

There has been quite a change recently in what I might call the philosophy of dog training. Emphasis has

swung away from what is termed compulsion training toward reward-only-based training. In simple terms, the latter is when you make a dog obey you with a reward instead of forcing it to obey you. A dog is encouraged to sit because you offer it a treat above its nose, rather than by physically pushing the dog into the sit position.

I don't take sides in this debate, although I do know that few dogs can be trained effectively by the average pet owner without there being some compulsion in their training methods. I apologize if this upsets the zealots but that's the way it is. Dog owners want results, not belief systems. Disciples of different training styles all too often become totally fixated on their approach to dog training to such a degree that, head in the sand, they only use positive reinforcement methods

THE CANINE MIND

of dog training, which simply do not work with all animals — especially difficult dogs.

The best illustration of this is the Recall — getting your dog to come to you in the park when it ignores you. Because these trainers have thrown out compulsive training methods, they may use a food treat, praise or toys to encourage the dog to come back to them. For example, I remember a real case with which I was involved. A dog called Spangle did not wish to come when he was having a terrific time in the park with his canine friends, chasing and pouncing upon other dogs that didn't relish his amorous intentions. The end result was that Spangle simply did not come when he was busy, despite the lure of chicken treats. The problem with dogs such as Spangle is that if the motivation to come to you is less appealing than the activity he is focused on, then obviously the dog will not come to you. Compelling the dog to come with actions that he doesn't like is now the only option. To look at it another way, you must interrupt what he is doing by making his current actions unpleasant or less fun.

As you progress through this book and follow the training program, you will see that we always use positive rewards in dog training; the trick is to use them in conjunction with other successful dog training techniques. If I thought juggling while standing on one leg would get dogs to successfully come on command, I would certainly give it a try! I will entertain any dog training method that is fair to both dog and owner.

Why Are Some Dogs Difficult to Train?

Dogs, like people, are a combination of many factors: their inheritance, their intelligence, their upbringing and breed-specific behaviors. Dogs that have learned the wrong behavior, or behavior that we find upsetting, will probably be more difficult to turn around than a young dog or puppy that's essentially a clean slate ready to learn good behavior. Whichever type or breed you own, don't worry — all dogs can be trained. I believe that most dogs are easy to train, and the rest just need extra tuition and instruction to bring them around. It's just a matter of how you perceive the dog and the amount of time you are prepared to devote to training it.

The Dog and its Innate Drives

In the wild, dogs have no naturally evolved instincts that encourage them to live with man or to be trained in obedience. *None*. The fact that by some quirk of history dogs have been domesticated and become our favorite companion is just fate. Like all wild animals, dogs need food, warmth and a stable environment to live in. Once

these basic needs have been met, dogs — like us — are essentially content.

A dog has a natural desire to stay with its pack. For a domesticated dog, this means you and your family. When you are outside together, a dog will stay within a certain distance of you. For most dog owners who live in suburbs or cities crisscrossed by roads, traffic and many other dangers, the distance from you that a dog needs to keep for safety is less than it would be in the wild. Even if you live in the country, the no-go areas are often just as plentiful. Farm livestock and crops pose different hazards for a country dog, but owners still have to keep their dogs away from them. So town and country dogs have different landscapes to traverse, but training is needed for both types of dog to control the pet and keep it out of danger.

Dogs have no sense of time or understanding of their owners' desires and routines. When they are disobedient and you become frustrated or angry, they do detect your change in mood but rarely appreciate the reasons behind it. So if you head out for an early morning walk with your dog, and then lose your temper when you find out that Rover has decided to run off in the opposite direction just when you want to get back home, remember that your rationalization is of little consequence to Rover. He's a dog. Of course, you're a human with your own emotions and this is the reason behind the clash of wills. With this book I will attempt to teach you how to get Rover back to you, but I cannot ever hope to convey to Rover the reasons why he must come,

except that there is always a reward from his leader. It is enough that he will recognize the fact that he has to come when called, and respond accordingly.

Some Common Training Problems

This section explores some of the common problems dog owners have to put up with in the real world. I have sat through thousands of consultations with clients listening to stories of their dogs' behavior, and can quickly get a feel for how dogs and owners develop love/hate relationships and how dog owners can be "taken in" by their dog's fawning antics in the evening by the fire. Yes, like children, dogs are nearly always forgiven for their mischievous behavior when tempers have cooled. I often think that dogs that we consider badly behaved probably learn very quickly that we humans blow hot and cold, and can nearly always be won over with a bit of paw offering. By the time you finish this book, this subtle piece of canine blackmail should be history.

COMMON PROBLEMS

Come Here

When taken out in the car or walked along the street and then released into an open space, many dogs become very excited. Why shouldn't they? For most dogs, this is the highlight of their otherwise uneventful day. A variety of scents, new canine friends to meet and fresh air racing through their lungs — these are the delights of the outside world in which they evolved. Although the park environment is man-made, dogs instinctively enjoy the short exhilarating high of running free.

Owners also love to see their dogs having a good time, but when the dog begins to sniff around the wrong dogs or to pester other park users, owners are often left looking embarrassingly helpless, trying to get their dog back by firmly voiced demands that inevitably degenerate into pleading gestures and outright begging. Eventually you may see them hauling their dog away from the target of interest, muttering "Bad dog!" or "That's it; you're not coming here again." That is, until evening relaxation time, when all is forgiven.

In the worst cases, dogs that don't come back can cause accidents in traffic and be a danger to one and all. So dogs do need to obey our commands despite their own canine agenda. Ultimately, they have to negotiate our world. The section on teaching the Recall in Chapter 10 will put you firmly in control of this important discipline.

The Pulling Battle

At Berkhamsted's Canine and Feline Behaviour Centre, I have a number of cameras in operation so that when clients arrive I am able to observe them get out of their vehicles along with their exuberant dogs. Just watching this brief episode conveys a good deal of information about the canine-human relationship in this pack.

Often the owner appears to be quite anxious, approaching the moment of letting their dog out of the car like going into battle. Suddenly a door is partially opened and the owner pounces on the dog and in the ensuing struggle a leash is attached. Then wham! — the dog is flying through the air, with the owner trying to brace themselves as they are hauled toward the consulting rooms.

I shouldn't, but I sometimes laugh at scenes like this, especially at the expressions on the owners' faces as they get dragged into the room muttering comments like "This is what I mean" or "That's it for you, Smokey, this man will sort you out." Then they smile a relieved smile as the dog, delirious with excitement, is gently attached by his leash to one of my wall hooks.

Dogs that pull are the bane of so many peoples' lives. In Chapter 8 I explain why dogs learn to pull — along with other related behaviors — and how to stop such pulling. Once this command is understood, the terrible choking sound of a dog frantic to get from A to B will also become a thing of the past.

Jumping Jack and Other Attention Seekers

Few people have not encountered a dog whose desire to get your attention involves launching themselves off the ground at your body and your face. The jumping dog is loved by some, hated by others but overall is an unwelcome pest, however well-intentioned its greetings may seem. Of course, all the reactions to a dog that jumps that I've just mentioned are a part of the problem behavior — inconsistent signals that confuse the animal. Do you recognize this behavior in your dog?

Your dog may not even jump, just nudge and demand your attention. Dogs are gregarious and, skilled in using wily ways to maintain or improve their position in the pack, quickly learn how to gain attention. This behavior is a form of dominance and is driven by the need to maintain a social position within your pack. Dogs obviously get a lot of pleasure from receiving attention, especially from a family superior — it demonstrates their own high status. But what about when excessive attention-seeking becomes annoying or the dog won't stop trying to get a response from a visitor who is not particularly dog-friendly or is not keen on a wet tongue lapping at their hands and face?

I shall tackle these problems in the Leadership Program in Chapter 3 and explain how you can control your dog through training and teach it good manners — well, good from a human perspective at least!

Common Laments of Owners of Untrained or Poorly Trained Dogs

- He's very obedient in the house.
- He's good on a walk — until he sees another dog or a person.
- He just loves people, but they sometimes get annoyed.
- He only pulls at the beginning of the walk.
- He's mad when I'm trying to put the leash on.
- He gets excited when he sees other animals.
- He can come when dinner's ready.
- He always comes back eventually.
- He doesn't always pull.
- He only jumps up when he first meets you.

What all these statements have in common is the inclination to excuse your dog's disruptive behavior and the fact that it will not obey you. We don't always like admitting our failings, so naturally we try and explain away the dog's bad behavior. Of course, as I often stress, the dog does not view any of its actions as bad. They are simply the sum of what it has learned despite our good intentions. But by using the training program outlined later in the book, these excuses can be laid to rest — our aim is to produce a well-trained dog that will consistently obey your commands.

CHAPTER TWO

What Is Dog Training?

Dog training means different things to different owners. For some it's a case of simply waiting for the right time and then joining a local club with their puppy and completing a course lasting about eight weeks. Other owners consider the matter easily solved by training their puppy or adult dog themselves. This is especially true of owners who have had dogs before — in other words, experienced dog owners.

Training dogs is open to all sorts of interpretation, and the different techniques that can be used often confuse the owner about to embark on training their dog. In addition, the dog has its own drives, which don't include walking endlessly in circles in a club. Dogs require motivational work to maintain their interest — just like people. I have trained many thousands of dogs from a very early age, and my experience has taught me a good deal about dog psychology, training methods, owners and their expectations and how they understand their dog.

A calm trainer with natural authority will be looked up to by his or her dog.

Dogs that are aggressive to other dogs or to people make life in the outside world difficult. Good obedience training brings such problems under control.

Moreover, I have trained more than 3,000 dogs in parks and public places with all the distractions that entails, and I sympathize with the ordinary dog owner who has difficulties controlling or training their dog in such places. Pragmatic and soundly based on experience, the knowledge I have acquired will be critical in giving you the best practical advice as you begin to train your dog.

The Behavioral Aspect of Training

Many people whose dogs cause them anguish own dogs with aggression problems. These problems may involve aggression toward people, other canines or both, and the situations can be complex. Yet while these dogs exhibit aggression, if the dog is trained to a high standard of obedience, a powerful element of control is introduced that can effectively stem, or at least control, the aggressive dog. Obedience will not convince the dog to like all the dogs or people it meets, but it will stop it from attacking by the simple fact that it will come, sit, lie down and stay when potentially troublesome situations arise. Once trained, an aggressive dog is easier to rehabilitate.

Dogs that have phobias or anxieties, who chase joggers or who are simply overboisterous can also be helped and controlled by dog training. An anxious dog is more likely to take a cue from a strong leader — you, the trainer. Your calmness and natural authority concentrates the dog's mind on you and what you are asking it to do. Of course these types of dogs still require behavior programs to calm their anxieties, but on the whole a well-trained dog is easier to manage. A dog that displays predatory chase behavior will also need to be taught deflections that redirect this behavior, but a strong recall taught well can stop the problem in the short term. Then you can work on redirecting the dog's desire to pursue sheep, cats, joggers or mail carriers.

The Well-Mannered Dog

Like a well-behaved child, obedience-trained dogs are certainly more welcome in most areas of our society. Although millions of us adore dogs, many

Well-trained dogs are welcome in the world at large as their behavior can be controlled.

people don't. So it is important for dog owners to give their dogs the best training possible. Unfortunately, human nature being what it is, too few people look at training as a preventive measure. Most people will purchase a book or video when a problem has already developed. This is like waiting for a car to break down before getting it serviced. Of course, unlike a car, a dog is a free-thinking, intelligent animal, and although a car may break down through lack of care, a dog will follow its own course of action if we do not teach it what we want it to do. The critical thing that breaks down is its behavior. That is why this book concentrates principally on solutions and training methods to help you to train your dog successfully.

It is a good idea to begin training when your puppy is quite young – I recommend training from the day you acquire the pup, when it is still at a very impressionable age.

TRAINING TECHNIQUES

The Challenges Awaiting You

You will be faced with a number of challenges, the first being to make sense of the conflicting claims of so many experts regarding the best way to train a dog. I hope to dispel any confusion and give clear advice on how to train your dog in a straightforward 21-day course. Practice thereafter will reinforce the training and help your dog to become a well-adjusted pet.

Owners will inevitably encounter media-savvy trainers offering miracles and results from the latest trends. They claim to use new ideas when, in fact, the principles of dog training have not really changed since the dog was first domesticated as a working animal. Their only novelty lies in the marketing lingo they use to sell their ideas. Such trainers constantly reinforce their own mystique and emphasize their special relationship with dogs, which they promise to share with you. This bait is used to hook you, the dog owner, as the dog itself is certainly not taken in by such grand claims. My skills are neither special nor unusually gifted, but come from the fact that I am passionate about dogs and learning

about them as a species. The old adage that practice makes perfect applies to dog training just as it does to any other skill in life. Dog training is not complicated or mysterious; it just involves learning another set of rules coupled with a desire to make proper contact with your dog — to forge a bond through a new language that we call "dog training."

Training Techniques

To be sure, over the years dog training techniques have improved and a more dog-friendly training philosophy has evolved that benefits both dogs and owners. We can now manipulate the dog's instincts and redirect those instincts into an activity that helps us train our dogs. For example, consider the dog's predatory behavior of chasing and catching prey. By substituting a ball for the prey and teaching the dog to pursue, catch and bring back the ball, the dog's instinctive love of the chase is partly satisfied. With repetition we can use the ball as an object that the dog craves. The ball is then used as a reward to teach a dog to sit, stand,

TRAINING AIDS

START : 1

Many dogs have an instinctive love of pursuit that you can turn to your advantage in training.

2

Playing chase and retrieve games with a ball or toy taps into the dog's innate desire to hunt prey.

COMMAND
"FETCH"

ie down and stay, and it even helps with recall exercises. It works in some, but not all, cases, which is why this book offers tried and tested methods in abundance. If one doesn't work, you can try another.

From a practical point of view, shepherds have been using this prey-catching instinct for hundreds of years, herding sheep by manipulating the same psychology of their dog's desire to hunt. The difference is that the herding dog brings back the sheep alive, not as his lunch! So although the principle is the same, the use has evolved into another aspect of dog training.

What Is a Trained Dog?

This question is open to much debate. My clients, who see me at Berkhamsted's Canine and Feline Behaviour Centre, have as many answers as the variety of breeds they bring to see me. The most common statement I hear is that their dog is trained, but just won't come back when there are distractions in the park, such as other dogs, squirrels or fascinating scents. So is the dog really trained? The dogs certainly know what "Come" means, as they obligingly demonstrate in the consulting rooms. This is what I call a convenient dog training response. In other words, if the dog has nothing more interesting to do, or if it has had its fun and is now a little tired, it will respond. That is not a trained dog. A trained dog is a dog that obeys you in all situations at your volition and command.

Very few people need a dog to come to them unless there is a good reason to command it to do so — perhaps the animal is bothering other dogs or park users, or running off toward a dangerously busy road. Dogs that only come of their own volition, not when they are commanded, regardless of what is on their mind, are not obedience-trained dogs. They are having more fun doing as they please. However, once they are trained, they can have just as much fun, but this time doing what you want them to do.

3
By repeating the game many times over, the dog comes to value the toy as it now associates it with the excitement of the chase game and the pleasure that it feels when its owner praises and strokes it for bringing the toy back.

COMMAND
"COME"

4
The favorite toy can now become a valuable training aid, being used as a treat to reward the dog for performing exercises like the Sit, Stand or Heel correctly.

TAKING CHARGE

Do We Need to Train Dogs?

Many of you reading this book would answer "yes." However, many people — too many — either can't be bothered or don't see dog training as important. Dogs, of course, vary immensely. Different breeds have their own instinctive behavior; collies are predisposed to chase, terriers can be feisty and cantankerous, while spaniels like to follow a trail of scent. Because of this innate variability, some dog owners do little in the way of training and get away with comparatively few problems, in the same way as some parents have an easy time when rearing an individual child. The fact that your dog naturally behaves well is not necessarily a reflection of

your skill. On the other hand, some clients of mine follow every rule in the book regarding puppy care and temperament development and still encounter severe difficulties in certain aspects of training that dog.

Dogs have very strong drives that can cause conflicts. For instance, over a period of years one client of mine has had different generations of the same breed of dog from the same breeder and the result of similar breeding lines. He used more or less the same approach to training each generation and yet had three different results. Chance obviously plays its part, so if you have tried really hard but your dog remains difficult, don't regard yourself as a failure. With this book, I will attempt to help you become a leader first, a trainer second and finally a dog owner who enjoys a close relationship with their dog.

The Leadership Program outlined in the next chapter is critical psychological training that should take place before the mechanics of obedience training begins. By following the program, you can psychologically take charge and teach your dog a very black-and-white style of obedience using a language that it understands and you can practice, and build a new positive relationship that is fair to the dog and you.

Try to make your children understand the dos and don'ts of training so that the dog is treated consistently by the whole family.

Dogs and Children

Training is important when dogs and children are likely to mix in the same family. A large number of dogs are purchased each year for children, and without a doubt dogs and other pets contribute a good deal to helping children understand the animal world.

If your children are interested and motivated, it is fun to include them in the training regime. But an adult should take control at first, so that the dog achieves a reasonable level of obedience before children enter the equation.

Dogs and children normally get along well together, but be careful — not all dogs are child-friendly!

Educated properly and using the ideas explained in this book, dogs can — and do — get along socially with children. However, the idea that all dogs love kids is a myth. Many dogs don't like children, especially small toddlers, particularly if the dog is already established in the home and the children come later. Their animated, unpredictable behavior can frighten a dog. So it is imperative that you select the right sort of dog and breed for your children's age group.

Training your dog to be obedient has a big effect on control of the dog, but it is equally vital to control your children around dogs. Once the child understands some of the elementary dos and don'ts of owning a dog, then even very young children can be allowed to take part in aspects of dog training. It's best to train your dog to a reasonable level first and then slowly allow your children to practice some of the training commands — starting with a few at a time. Children's delivery of commands can be hit and miss at first — especially with regard to consistency — but older children soon catch on, and then they too can enjoy training the dog and building up basic control skills.

Children over the age of about ten can be allowed to walk dogs, but the safety rule I always bear in mind is: if the dog panics or needs restraint, could the child hold back the dog physically? So consider the size of your dog in relationship to the child before letting them take it out for a walk, however trained it may be. Safety first.

CHAPTER THREE

The Leadership Program

We often treat dogs like people. We are sometimes ridiculed for doing this, while at other times we are admired for having such a good relationship with our dog. I feel that if people wish to indulge their dogs in this way, that is up to them, but there are negative consequences if you forget that a dog is a dog. Dogs that are spoiled can become confused as to where they fit into the hierarchy of the human pack, and as a result, your ability to effectively train the dog is compromised.

It's human nature to be kind to a family member, even when that member has four legs and wags its tail. However, when we are trying to train a dog to fit into our household and the wider world outside and we expect the dog to obey us, it will only behave as the natural instincts of the species dictate. I must emphasize that spoiling a dog and overindulging it can make training that dog much harder. As the saying goes, "Treat a dog like a person and it will treat you like a dog." So don't set yourself up for disappointment.

The Wolf in Your House

The wolf's nature and patterns of behavior are present within your dog irrelevant of breed, however altered its behavior may seem as a result of domestication. The rules that govern the hierarchical order and smooth functioning of the wolf pack are the rules that your dog understands, and it is the dominant or deferential positions by which wolves communicate that we are going to use to help you train your dog. This is what I mean by stressing the use of canine psychology, as well as repetitive dog training exercises to achieve our goals. In the introduction I described the dog's natural drives — by manipulating these we can psychologically demote our dog, or at least teach it that it has to respect you as the leader and the rest of your family as higher-ranking members of your family pack.

Now it may seem that your dog is quite deferential already, but most dogs have learned how to manipulate people to suit their own ends. More often than not we are unaware of our dog's determination to control situations in a daily routine. This can be something as simple as barging through doors first or seemingly as innocuous as demanding free attention. These dominant/demanding behaviors by themselves may appear harmless, but combined with other behaviors they can build up the dog's rank within your family pack. We call this dominant behavior, a term that despite its strong overtones does not mean aggressive.

Labradors and boxers, for example, often exert considerable dominance over their owners; we often put it down to the fact that the dog is large and used to throwing its weight around. To make life easier, we either put up with such behavior or simply work around the boisterousness, even if the dog knocks you out of the way as it bolts to get to the door first. Toy breeds may not use size and weight to assert dominance, but use other cunning attention-seeking tactics, such as demanding to be picked up at will. Over a period of time dogs like this can take over the leader's role that many of us unwittingly vacate. This does not make the dog bad; it is just a dog doing what its innate drives prompt it to do when living with a pack of humans that are giving it vague and unreadable signals. The golden rule is: lead or be led. Now is the time to assert yourself and treat the dog in such a way that it will find a comfortable place at the bottom of the family pack. Contrary to popular belief, when frustrated dog owners scream, bellow and get angry with their dogs, the behavior simply conveys to the dog the fact that that we may shout and be angry. They do not understand why.

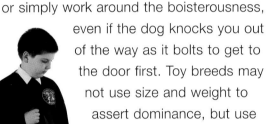

How Does this Affect Training?

A dog that does not see you as a leader tends not to listen unless doing so suits its own purpose. Dogs that don't listen are more difficult to train and can get themselves into all sorts of conflict with us and the wider world around us.

Even if your dog does not appear to be high ranking, the Leadership Program will still help define many aspects of your relationship and enhance your ability to command obedience. It reduces any ambiguity in the rapport between you and your dog, establishes clear boundaries, and helps the dog to listen and learn. The dog training you are about to embark upon will speed up many times over if you implement the Leadership Program outlined below first.

The essence of the program is to remove a good deal of the time and affection we devote to our dogs when they demand it, but give back that praise, touch, attention and affection when it is linked to the learning of an action that we want them to perform. In this training, we are not totally denying the dog rewards, simply redistributing our kindness and attention. Any action that the dog uses to get us to defer to it is also ignored, as is any behavior that gives the dog an elevated view of its position within the family pack.

*During the Leadership Program, strokes, pats and attention are only given to a dog when **you** choose to do so. You, the trainer, lead the pack.*

THE HOME FRONT

The House Plan

The Leadership Program involves you taking actions that psychologically demote your dog and establish your own superiority in the domestic pecking order. The program begins at home, and is best introduced over a one-week period before beginning the 21-day training program.

We spend most of our time in the home with our dogs. Some of you will already have designated areas where your dog can and cannot go — others will have no such rules and allow their dog free run of the house or apartment at will. Some dogs will be allowed into the bedroom, while others will have their own bed in the hall, kitchen or other similar room in the house. While I don't want to judge the rights or wrongs of your personal wishes, I must clearly state that if you want to train your dog well, you will need to treat it like a dog and make sure that you call the shots in your own home. Moreover, once the dog understands the new rules, it will become calmer and more obedient as you develop your role as leader.

To put the Leadership Program into practice, you must take control of your living space and draw up clear rules as to where the dog can and cannot go.

The Bedroom

The bedroom is attractive to many dogs because they can spend long periods of time there next to the leader, thereby giving them a very important privilege and, by extension, high rank. Your scent is powerful in this room and you — the leader — sleep here. It is noticeable that dogs will often choose to sleep in the company of the adult members of the family rather than in the children's bedrooms. Some people place a basket in the bedroom, but from the dog's point of view the room is the important element. It's not just the basket or bed, it's the location and your presence there. So if your dog sleeps in your bedroom, ban it from now on. This helps demonstrate to your dog that you are the leader.

I also recommend that you refrain from letting the dog sleep on landings or stairways. Install a childproof gate to help you to enforce this rule without endlessly repeating orders and telling the dog off constantly for trying to go where it had previously been allowed. Like all the rules that follow, initially this will be confusing for the dog, but that's the way it is. They will soon adapt to the change and become better dogs in the process.

The Living Room

If your dog has access to the living room or the main room in your house, make this room off limits as well. By excluding the dog for most of the time that you are relaxing in the living room, the dog again has his lower rank emphasized. Do allow the dog in periodically; perhaps play a game of ball and at the end of the game put the ball in a secure box and let the dog see you doing it. Then relax and only call him to you for a stroke when you choose to do so. Of course that stroke is not for free — it is a reward for him coming on command. Then tell him to sit or lie down for a while and praise him accordingly. Keep everything calm — no long, excited pats and strokes. After about half an hour or so the dog must leave the living room when told for its usual place in the kitchen, hallway or garden.

If you are using the hook restriction program (see page 28), install several hooks in different rooms to help you when you are first using them as a tool to teaching the dog to stay out of your living room.

Easy Chairs

Dominant dogs, like their counterparts in the wild, like to occupy elevated positions and especially positions that we habitually take as our own. In a house that means the couch, comfortable chairs in the living room and even, in the case of smaller dogs, your lap. Many people even set aside an old chair for the dog as a way of keeping it off their other furniture. My response to this is a big **"No."** Dogs that are given these privileges, and even a chair for themselves, feel entitled to assume the appropriate status. This again removes the line of demarcation between the leader and the led. Dogs love surveying their territory from on high and allowing them on chairs also makes them assume that they can have access to the main room when it suits them, as opposed to being invited to enjoy the privilege. So ban the dog from these places and teach it to get off the furniture. You are the leader and the dog must go only where you allow.

Occupying a favorite chair is one of the ways that a dog seeks to assert high rank in the domestic environment.

OFF THE CHAIR!

Things have to change. You must instruct the dog to get off the chair and forbid it from enjoying that privilege from now on. This is all part of the plan to demote the dog and promote yourself as pack leader.

RIGHTS OF PASSAGE

Out of My Way

Have you noticed how dogs often decide to sleep or nap in the most inconvenient place, such as the middle of a doorway or in a hall? Sometimes it's simply comfortable for the dog, but many dogs notice how we — as caring owners — tiptoe around them. Even when we tell them to move, many dogs do so reluctantly or ignore you completely. After a while it becomes the norm. This has to stop. Your dog instinctively knows that a leader would make it get out of the way. When a leader walks tall, the other pack members make way. So when walking around the house, make your dog get out of your way. If the dog will not move by command, then slowly shuffle your feet toward it and as they touch the dog, it should move. Don't say "Good boy" — just walk on by. For obstinate dogs I often push a vacuum or broom ahead of me as I go, so the dog gets the message. The dog quickly realizes it must move when any family member wants to walk past and it also learns not to lie in certain places. It's good manners and helps to teach the dog that you are the leader. "Make way for the leader" is the order of the day.

Doors and Gates

Many dogs like to push their way ahead of us through doors or when a gate is opened. Again owners can get used to these ploys, often to such an extent that we sometimes see people waiting for their dog to go through an open door first, saving them from being knocked out of the way by the excited mutt. Little dogs will sometimes zoom in and then come charging back out again all at once. If your dog is one of these types, this behavior has to stop now. Why? Well, the leader leads. Even in human society people of rank go first; in canine society it is the absolute rule that the leader should always go first. Wolves often trot in line in order of rank.

If your dog tries to surge ahead, simply slam the door quickly shut so that it cannot go ahead of you. Open the door slightly and ease your body through first, then call the dog on command. If it tries to push through in an undisciplined way, slam the door again, making sure not to hit the dog. The loud noise of the door banging shut should sufficiently startle it. Repeat as many times as necessary. If your dog is particularly large or determined, or both, you can use a collar and leash for added control, and maybe have another family member on hand to help. It's time-consuming in the short term, but after a week or so you'll have an obedient, well-mannered dog at your side and no more bruises on your legs.

Feeding Your Dog

Try to feed your dog after you have enjoyed your main meal of the day. Your dog's acute sense of smell will immediately tell it that food is being prepared, although it is not getting any — not even a tidbit or leftovers.

START : 1

If you have a dog that habitually lies on the floor around the house and is reluctant to get out of your way as you go about your day-to-day business, you've got a leadership problem.

COMMAND
"MOVE"

OUT OF MY WAY!

2
Go up to the dog and "walk tall." It is time to assert your rank. No more stepping over or around the motionless animal.

3
Command the dog to move out of your way. If that doesn't work, shuffle forward with both feet.

COMMAND
"MOVE"

4
The dog will move when it feels your feet. Don't stop to praise it, just walk on by.

Leaders of the pack eat first. Wait about 30 minutes after you have eaten and then feed your dog. Dogs are not grazers and do not need to eat several times a day. Thereafter teach your dog to sit and wait to eat; it should only be allowed to start on your say-so. I simply use the command **"Yours"** or **"Eat."**

Tidbits, Treats and Food

Don't allow your dog to beg and scrounge food from the table. Better still, don't allow it anywhere near your eating area. It will get the message that the leaders not only eat first, but don't allow lower pack members near them. This is a strong visual and olfactory signal that your dog will note. Because we use food a good deal in training, don't offer the dog any treats except when advised to do so during the training programs — otherwise you will make life harder for yourself and remove the motivation for the dog. Some dogs are exceptions to the rule and are always hungry, but not all are like this.

Toys and Balls

As with food, remove all the dog's toys for the immediate future, and especially if you are going to use them as motivators during training. A toy is not such a delight for a dog in training if it can play with the same toy any time it chooses. Discover the toy that your dog likes most and use that in training. Lock the rest away. Possessions mean a lot to dogs. When you take control of them and determine how and when they are used, the dog will again be impressed with your leadership behavior.

Ignore those beseeching looks and lock away all the dog's toys for the duration of the program. We want to use the dog's pleasure in play as a powerful motivator in the training exercises.

NO FREE REWARDS

Petting and Stroking

This is the most difficult area on which to advise dog owners. I don't want you to stop petting your dog, but I want you to stop doing it for free or when your dog demands it. I realize this is anathema to many people who love their dogs and I concede that there is little point in having a dog if you can't pet it or enjoy its company. Well, just bear with me on this one. It's not denial forever — just part of a short-term strategy to make training easier and to help build up a healthy relationship with your dog.

Dogs love affection and touch. Like us, they are very tactile and it's this natural desire for close pack association that I will be exploiting in all of the dog training exercises in this book. In fact, if you train three times a day as I advise and play games and walk your dog in combination with the training, then the amount of attention, touch and petting the dog receives will be quite considerable. The difference is that now it's simply being linked to training and is no longer idle contact. Often my clients lament that they suffer more than their dogs when doing this. I believe them. Dogs soon realize that the withdrawal and redistribution of attention just means that rewards arrive in new ways. They adjust quickly and don't dislike you for it — they don't hold a grudge like us. Feeling bad is simply an expression of our guilt, and dogs don't relate to guilt.

The Ignore

It will be difficult to abstain from petting and stroking your dog. It's quite natural when people are relaxing in a room to see pet dogs occasionally walking up to someone for attention or a casual stroke. Many dogs, especially the smaller breeds, have got human social dynamics figured out and spend half the night comfortably nestled in laps, being treated like a Roman emperor. These dogs are clever and have achieved a

Dogs love it when we fuss over them. We can put this to good use in training.

very high status. Yes, stroking dogs is good for us and the dogs certainly like it, but for the training to succeed we need to review these routines.

Unfortunately, from now on the rule is: **Ignore it!** No more sitting on laps and no more strokes or attention for free. I know it is hard and that you feel bad. Good! If you feel bad, you are probably following my advice really well. And, as mentioned earlier, you will be able to offer your dog plenty of attention through the training exercises later. If your dog

It's tempting to stroke a dog that's begging for attention, but you must learn to curb your desire and ignore it.

loves your attention, it will love dog training. Don't view the new rules as "punishment" either — it's just a change of regime for a few months.

Dog Training and the Leadership Program

By far the most useful and impressive way to be a leader is to train your dog, and the Leadership Program helps you to do this. Very few dogs that are well trained and treated as dogs (rather than surrogate humans) display any problematic behavior. Dogs that first understand what you want them to do and then obey **all** — not some — of your commands are showing you their lower position within the family pack and are less likely to challenge your leadership. Your ability to command and your dog's willingness to obey prevents most disputes — this is beneficial to dog and owner alike and improve the quality of everyone's life.

Length of the Program

Each year I place about 500 of my clients' dogs on this program and many thousands more experience it through my video and television programs. Without exception, the clients excitedly tell me of the positive changes

Strokes and tidbits are now dispensed as part of the rewards for training obediently.

they observe in their dogs' behavior, and that's before they begin the actual dog training. They admonish their dogs very little, and the dogs seem so keen and obedient. They say things like "I can't believe how quickly the dog has changed and improved. It's wonderful." That's because it works — you are using a language that dogs innately understand. You are becoming a true leader and dogs always feel more secure with a strong leader — they are less likely to challenge your commands and, like children, they will feel more comfortable knowing the boundaries of what is and isn't permitted.

Rewards must be earned.

Once your dog has been fully trained to the standard you require, during the following months you can begin to relax some of the rules, especially those governing stroking, attention and being in your company. You will have taught the dog obedience, which is a new language, and communication, which improves your relationship. Conflict is minimal and harmony should reign. If your dog appears to be backpedaling, you may have relinquished your grip a bit too soon. This is especially likely with very dominant dogs of any size or breed. Dogs that are naturally lower ranking by nature are less problematic and privileges can be reintroduced more rapidly.

Which rules you choose to relax is really a matter of personal choice. I personally don't allow my dogs on furniture or beds at any time for practical hygiene reasons, and I maintain all the above rules for my dogs for life with the exception of general affection and access to my living room.

HOOK RESTRICTION

The Hook — A Restriction Program for the Dominant Dog

In the previous section I referred to the problems of dealing with dogs that are dominant by nature. The dominant dog poses particular problems of its own, and that is where the hook restriction program can be helpful.

Many people complain that they cannot control their dog when visitors arrive. Chaos reigns as they try to stop the dog from jumping up and knocking into the visitors. The journey from the front door to the living room can seem interminable as everyone tries to make headway as the dog blocks the route and jumps around demanding endless attention. Of course, good obedience training will prevent most of this, but in the short term I also use hook restriction training. This utilizes a sturdy metal hook that is attached to a metal base plate, which can be securely screwed to a wall. It's like a child's playpen without bars and certainly helps to control boisterous dogs. It also prevents dogs from believing that they can inspect, pester or impose on each and every friend or visitor who might visit your home. Teaching your dog to go to its bed or living area is also useful, but in the early stages the hook training system gives the dog no choice.

Equip yourself with a Kong toy (a hollow rubber dog toy that can be stuffed with food) and a hook fixed to a suitable wall or baseboard. I also use a chain leash about 1 m (3 ft.) in length with a dog clip at its end. (The length will depend on your dog's size.) Every day place the dog on the hook by slipping the end of the leash over it and put a small quantity of its daily food allowance in the rubber toy. This teaches the dog to associate the restriction of being on the hook with the pleasure of gnawing away at the Kong. Most dogs will complain about this new regime by barking and performing other antics, but simply ignore the dog and only release it when it is calm. The beauty of the toy is that it takes time for the dog to extract the food, which in turn gives the dog an extended reward associated with the hook. After about a week of experiencing this new system, most dogs gladly walk to the hook with you and accept the new training.

Once taught, hook restriction can be used as a safety measure if you have workers entering your home and you don't want your dog to get outside. It's also good when the dog is overexcited, or when people arrive and the dog won't leave them alone. I always use it when the doorbell rings to prevent the boisterous dog problem. It saves all that shouting, annoyance and disturbance to your visitors. In time the training should prove effective and the dog will learn to go to the front door with you on a collar and leash and obediently escort your friends into your home. On your command, it can then receive some praise from them in the appropriate fashion.

Dogs enjoy the time that they spend on the hook while coaxing food out of a food toy.

Summary of the Hook Restriction Program

How the hook can help deal with the problem of a dominant dog that overwhelms visitors:

1 When visitors call, place your dog on its leash and collar.
2 Use collar and leash for control and place the end of the leash over the hook.
3 If the dog barks incessantly, use a second hook in another room — ignore the dog.
4 Instruct guests to ignore your dog, and that includes even looking at it.
5 Once all is calm — no barking or whining for about 15 minutes — release the dog.
6 You and your guests must not acknowledge the dog until it has settled down quietly.
7 If the dog brings toys and uses other ploys to obtain attention, ignore these too.
8 A powerful reward for behaving well is the Release, but only do it when your dog is quiet.
9 If you approach your dog to release it and it starts to become overexcited, walk away.
10 The dog will learn over time that calmness brings reward and release.

Now let's review what the dog has learned:

Behavior Denied
• Dashing to the front door is no longer allowed — reward removed.
• Pushing family or visitors is no longer acceptable — reward removed.
• Imposing on people who are sitting or constantly demanding petting is now forbidden — reward removed.

• Acting in an excessively boisterous way has stopped — reward removed.

New Learning
• Being on the hook tether is now rewarded with a toy stuffed with food.
• Being released only happens when the dog is not over-excited — the reward is being released.
• Walking quietly around people is rewarded with a stroke. Jumping up isn't.
• Shouting and threats from irritated people are things of the past.
• Learning some obedience commands and behaving accordingly produces more rewards.

When you reach this stage, you will have a dog that is truly receptive to training. The peaceful, calm atmosphere allows dog and owner to communicate in a language that is clear, and the dog is now ready to learn new positive exercises. Just as the chaos in a classroom run by a poor teacher struggling with unruly children changes into a more orderly and pleasant atmosphere when someone skilled takes charge, so a calm and attentive dog is ready for training.

CHAPTER FOUR

Puppy Obedience Training

In this chapter I will explore tips for training puppies over six weeks old. With puppies, we certainly need to be less formal in our training compared to how we teach adult dogs, and, above all, we must be more patient with a pup. While the training section of this book does allude to puppy training, the extra ideas in this chapter will specifically help you train your puppy.

Puppies, like children, vary in the speed of their mental and physical development through to maturity. Moreover, because there are many different breeds with various traits, puppies train at different speeds. In general, the giant breeds mature more slowly than the smaller breeds. Some breeders will allow puppies to leave the litter at six weeks of age; others will not. On average, puppies become available at around eight weeks; don't accept a puppy older than this if you wish to have the best chance of socializing it into your lifestyle. Of course, there are exceptions where a breeder has socialized the puppy properly in a house and then allowed it into the outside world with relevant precautions, but the general eight-week rule holds true.

One or Two Puppies?

At first this may seem a sensible idea, but avoid purchasing two puppies together, even though some breeders remark how wonderful this can be. It's not. It simply makes training much more difficult — not because twice the amount of training is required, but because the two pups will form a little pack and constantly compete with one another. Their natural attention will not be focused on you. If you want two dogs, buy one first, fully train it to adulthood and then bring in a second. This also makes it easier to train the second pup, which will tend to copy the actions of the older trained dog and learn a great deal by association. As you will have already accumulated considerable knowledge and skill through your experience of training the first dog, this arrangement makes training much easier.

Two puppies look sweet, but it is easier to train one puppy at a time.

Personality

If you have purchased a puppy with a very strong character or one that exhibits dominant behavior, you can implement the Leadership Program described in the previous chapter, making sensible alter-ations when necessary to take the puppy's age into account. This will certainly help the dominant puppy learn its place in your family pack. It is easier to set ground rules early on, rather than trying to alter the dog's behavior later on when it is fully grown. I personally like strong-minded dogs, and simply redirect that energy and character through dog training.

Puppies do not normally arrive with bad habits. They are just naturally inquisitive with their normal innate drives — you can quickly manipulate this curios-ity to suit your training purposes and to help ensure the pup's future stability and welfare. Ignore anyone who tells you that puppies should be trained when they are older. This simply will not work. Puppies can — and do — learn from day one in your home. It's up to you whether you decide to lead that training by direct-ing its natural curiosity into learning all the behavior that helps it enjoy a happy adult life, or let the puppy learn on its own by trial and error, which will lead to a good deal of conflict with you.

Puppies will learn from a well-trained older dog.

The Mind of a Pup

I suggest that you regard a puppy as you would a two-year-old child — innocent of all actions. It does not know guilt or malice; it is simply driven by basic instincts and the desire to fit in with its new pack, however non-dog-like they appear.

Certain exercises described in this book can be used for puppies and are marked puppy-friendly. This doesn't mean that you cannot use the other exercises — merely that it's sensible to try to teach the puppy using a positive approach in the first instance. This also doesn't mean the puppy cannot be disciplined when necessary, or you cannot use training discs (see page 42), a water pistol or other items to reinforce your training if everything else is not working. Avoiding a clash is better than waiting for the inevitable to happen.

A puppy's concentration span can be quite short. So limit any lesson to at most five minutes in duration — pups are easily distracted and are physically incapable of maintaining the Stay position for more than a few seconds. Until the puppy is about four months of age, it is best to concentrate on trying to drive home the ideas and actions you want the puppy to learn and perform, rather than be overconcerned about exactness. The exceptions are mouthing (using its teeth on you) and chewing any item that may be dangerous.

STARTING TO TRAIN

Puppy Training Plan

The puppy training plan on page 35 is a guide to what you can achieve. It's not set in stone; depending on the breed, a puppy's speed of progress will vary. I find that a dog trainer who is an opportunist generally reaches a much higher standard with a puppy than one that concentrates too much on formal discipline.

For example, when a puppy is in its playpen or appointed room in the house, you can introduce it to toys to encourage mind-stimulating activity as well as channel its energies and sense of inquisitiveness into play, so that it chews the right things instead of the leg of the kitchen chair. Squeaky toys really excite many puppies as they seem to

A squeaky toy is ideal for teaching a puppy recall lessons. Learning is wrapped up in an enjoyable game.

*Puppies love to jump up at their owners in an attempt to get close to their faces. In the wild, young dogs use this tactic as a way of getting older dogs to regurgitate food for them. In training you can redirect this movement and encourage the puppy to fall back into a **"Sit"** position.*

imitate the sounds of prey animals. I sometimes use the toy around the kitchen and when I want to teach the Recall I'll squeak the toy and command **"Come"** simultaneously, then praise the puppy or reward it with a tidbit when it responds.

As puppies are so small, they have to look up to see our faces. In the wild the distance between a wild dog's head and that of a puppy is much smaller. A puppy in the wild will seek face-to-face contact with an adult dog in order to ask for food that the mature dog will then regurgitate. Despite the disparity in size between a puppy and its human owner, the pup will still try to get to your mouth for food.

When they rush up to you, try holding the toy, a food tidbit or just your outstretched fingers above the puppy. It will often fall into a Sit position as it concentrates its vision on the focus point — immediately when this happens give the command **"Sit"** and treat the pup with a reward. I use the same motivational techniques to teach other disciplines, like the Down.

Introduction of the Leash and Collar

First attach the puppy's collar around its neck and leave it for a few days so that it can get used to it. Initially it may scratch it, as the collar feels unnatural. Some puppies get used to the new collar right away. After a few days attach a 1–1.2 m (3–4 ft.) leash to the collar but don't try to walk the puppy as you would an

Immediately drop the leash to release the tension and allow the puppy to drag it. After a few seconds pick up the leash again and continue training. A few minutes per session are all that is needed, repeated five or six times daily. Practice the same routines in the yard. Only when the puppy is not fearful of the leash and collar should you attempt to walk in public places.

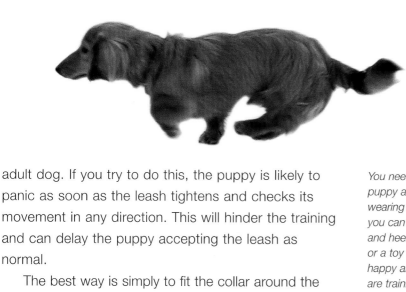

adult dog. If you try to do this, the puppy is likely to panic as soon as the leash tightens and checks its movement in any direction. This will hinder the training and can delay the puppy accepting the leash as normal.

The best way is simply to fit the collar around the puppy's neck while sitting on the floor with a small bag of tidbits, such as tiny bits of cheese or ham, on hand. When the puppy runs around, offer it a tidbit as a distraction. At some point the pup will run off to the full length of the leash and be brought to a halt. Take its mind off the sudden tightening by moving your arm to give the leash more slack while offering the pup a tidbit as a distraction. Puppies quickly recover their sense of curiosity and will start playing again. A toy will also act as a distraction from the leash tightening.

Next, walk around the room, offering the pup tidbits or the toy while trying your best to keep the leash loose. Slowly the puppy will get used to the restriction caused by the collar and leash. If the pup suddenly darts off and the leash abruptly tightens, it may panic — this is natural.

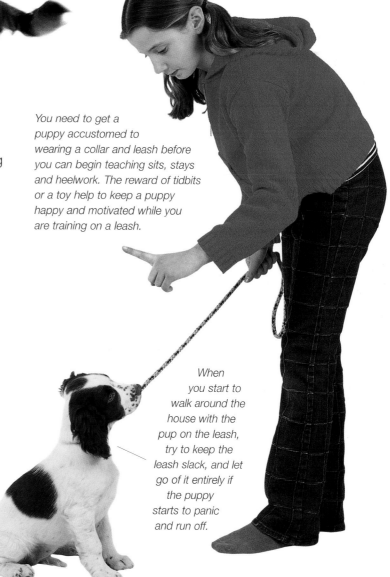

You need to get a puppy accustomed to wearing a collar and leash before you can begin teaching sits, stays and heelwork. The reward of tidbits or a toy help to keep a puppy happy and motivated while you are training on a leash.

When you start to walk around the house with the pup on the leash, try to keep the leash slack, and let go of it entirely if the puppy starts to panic and run off.

TRAINING PLAN

Sit and Down Stays

When teaching puppies to stay, it is best to use a leash and collar for control. Initially concentrate on teaching the puppy to stay for about five seconds or so and then increase this to around 30 seconds over a week or so, while moving a few steps away. The length of time for which a puppy stays is not the important point — what you are trying to do is to instill the idea of the Stay. Puppies find staying for long a little too much for their concentration levels. Physically they tend to roll over, flop and suddenly take off in a playful run. This is not disobedience; it's like a child being suddenly attracted to something else in its immediate world. Persevere and congratulate yourself on succeeding when you manage to achieve small increments. Punishment is generally not required. Try to guide the puppy sympathetically, rather than putting it in circumstances where it is likely to get into mischief and then blaming the puppy for being naughty. For practical reasons, I don't introduce the Stand position until the pup is about 12 weeks of age.

In the garden or park, puppies shouldn't be let off the leash to run free. They may look cute and attract attention from admiring passers-by, but they must learn that it is normal for you to be in control. This is the time for the puppy, however young, to learn to concentrate on you. It only takes a few admirers to crouch down and let the puppy jump up at them for stroking for it to learn that jumping on people is very rewarding. These same people won't be so amused six months later when a 25 kg (55 lb.) Weimaraner remembers this little game and launches itself at them.

I use a flexi-leash in the yard or park to begin recall training using the same methods as for adult dogs. Use inducements like food rewards to encourage your

pup to train. These will suffice in most cases; however, for the older puppy or one that is persistently reluctant to come for any of the rewards, I jerk the leash gently, but just sufficiently enough to interrupt the pup. This is not meant to hurt it or pull it back to me. When the pup's head pops up to see what that tug was for, I quickly call it to me excitedly. Long lines or flexi-leashes are very important when safety is required. Using a line

STAND
Don't introduce the stand until week three – pups find it harder.

SIT
You can use a tidbit to encourage a puppy to fall back into the Sit.

DOWN
Don't ask a puppy to stay for too long – they tend to lose concentration.

does not preclude using toys, food and your own ability to dramatically attract your pup's attention and encourage its interest in coming to you. We are simply establishing early conditioning of the lessons we want the puppy to learn in the future.

Puppy socialization and training classes abound in most cities. If run well, they can help you socialize your puppy. Run badly, they can traumatize your puppy and damage its temperament for good. Go and observe how a class is run. If things seem orderly, the instructor has control over the more exuberant puppies, and all the puppies seem happy and full of fun, then let your puppy play, mix and say hello to other pups.

PUPPY TRAINING PLAN

Puppies should be taught the following exercises over approximately a five-minute period. Aim to repeat the training three or four times a day. You can use any of the methods marked Puppy Safe in the training section of the book.

WEEK 1	WEEK 2	WEEK 3
Sit	**Sit**	**Sit**
Down	**Down**	**Down**
Heel	**Heel**	**Heel**
Sit/Stay for about five seconds	**Sit/Stay** for up to 10 seconds	**Stand** introduction
Down/Stay for about five seconds	**Down/Stay** for up to 10 seconds	**Sit/Stay** for up to 20 seconds
Recall on a leash, several times	**Recall** on a flexi- or longer leash, several times	**Down/Stay** for up to 30 seconds
		Recall off leash in the yard and around the house, several times

PUPPY TRAINING DOS AND DON'TS

DOS

- Puppies train best after they have just woken from a nap.
- Puppies are very much food-oriented, so tiny pieces of ham, cheese and chicken are welcome in training.
- Use motivational methods — they help to teach the Come.
- For recall, introduce a whistle and voice command — later on, it helps with training in the park.
- Train the pup to heel around the home and garden, not just when you are able to go to the park.
- Play plenty of games with puppies during training and after the lessons. Games create good associations between you and the training periods.

DON'TS

- Don't use the hook restriction program (see page 28) with puppies — they can get tangled up and panic.
- Don't hit a puppy. If you get frustrated, try training later on when you are calmer. Remember the puppy has no idea what you are trying to achieve.
- Don't train to the point of exhausting the pup — their brains cannot cope with too much training at once.

CHAPTER FIVE

Training Equipment

Dog training equipment is relatively inexpensive to buy considering how much you can achieve with it when it is used knowledgeably. However, it's important not to waste money on unsuitable collars and leashes; avoid chain-plated and fancy leashes and collars adorned with spikes or studs. A long 1.2 m or 2 m (4 ft. or 6 ft.) leash made of fine leather or quality nylon is all you need. For collars I prefer smooth, round leather. Don't get a chain or items that can choke a dog when pulled tight. Dog training collars are fine as they have a limiting device that prevents them from overtightening.

Some of the equipment I recommend here is intended to be used on dogs that are proving more difficult to train or on dogs that have already been inappropriately trained and have fallen into bad habits. The face collar is one item that provokes differing reactions. Some people who have endured their dog's traumatic introduction to a face collar and consequently stopped using it condemn it as useless. However, when used and introduced properly, I consider the face collar to be a clever and valuable dog-training aid. It is described in more detail later in this chapter.

Here's a basic list of equipment that you will need for training your dog:

- A 1.2 m (4 ft.) leash and also a 2 m (6 ft.) one if you can get both (leather is best)
- A collar, either a standard fixed one that cannot tighten fully, or a dog training collar
- A long line about 10 m (33 ft.) in length made of thin strong nylon
- A short line about 2 m (6 ft.) in length
- A flexible leash, especially useful with puppies

As well as these basics, there are many other items available that can prove useful. These options are outlined in more detail below.

Dog Body Harnesses

There are a number of dog body harnesses on the market and they are useful when traveling with your dog in a car. They work similar to a child harness. Always place your dog in the back seat if possible and fix the harness straps onto the seat belt for safety. Dogs that ride in a car this way are less likely to misbehave and when car doors are opened the dog cannot leap out.

These harnesses are not appropriate for teaching dogs to heel (not to pull on the lead). For this you need a walking harness.

Dog Walking Harnesses

These harnesses are specifically designed to teach dogs to heel by making pulling on the leash uncomfortable. They work by causing uncomfortable pressure under the dog's "armpits" under its front legs when it

Walking harnesses are designed to exert an uncomfortable pressure under the front legs of dogs that try to surge ahead of their handlers.

surges ahead — if the dog stops pulling there is no pressure on the sensitive skin surface in its leg pits. They work effectively on many dogs and don't require much skill on the handler's part.

Reasons to Use
- Heel training
- Restraint

Flexible Leash Training (puppy safe)

A flexible leash (flexi-leash) has many uses in training a dog. It is a long leash that extends and rewinds into a small plastic container with a handle. It has a button near the handle that locks the line at any chosen position. Pressing the button again releases the line, which is reeled in onto a spool by a spring. It's a good control device to use with young puppies when they are first being trained and it safely keeps them under your control up to a distance of about 12 m (40 ft.), depending on the model used.

The flexi-leash also helps when introducing a pup to another dog or a house cat — it allows the animal some freedom while you still retain control of the leash.

Reasons to Use
- Prevents dogs from running off while offering them some freedom
- Sometimes used for the stay and recall exercises
- Behavior lessons when introducing other pets

Long Lines

The long line is primarily used for the recall exercise and is made from thin strong nylon. It can be between 6 and 15 m (20 and 50 ft.) long. Hardware or pet stores often sell it. Simply fix a dog hook at one end to attach to the collar and make a handling loop at the other. The line can be tough on the hands, so it pays to wear thick gloves when using a long line for recall training.

Reasons to Use
- Recall training
- Stays
- Helps stop dogs from pursuing livestock by teaching recall

A flexible lead unwinds and rewinds into a plastic reel to which a handle is attached. It is useful when training puppies to heel.

COLLARS

Face Collars

Face collars help stop dogs pulling: of all the heel training aids, other than heel training itself, they are the most effective. But they are often actively rejected by the dog at first and this can upset the owner. The device fits over the dog's muzzle and head, and allows the dog's mouth to open as usual so that it can breathe properly. When the dog pulls ahead of the owner, the head collar redirects the dog's head back to the owner's side, thereby making it uncomfortable and awkward for the dog to pull. It teaches the dog that walking alongside you on a loose leash is the most comfortable option for him.

Face collars are particularly good for large dogs or when the owner is not particularly mobile or able to control a powerful dog that pulls strongly. Face collars also have a calming effect on some overboisterous dogs. Many dogs freak out when you first place a face collar on them. They may rub their faces on the floor and appear very alarmed. Well, they are alarmed, but the dramatics are greater than the actual experience merits. The distress that some dogs feel can be reduced by the way you introduce the collar, explained below. This distress is only a short-term reaction in most cases; I feel that it is better for a dog to come to terms with this than to spend its time choking on all its walks for the rest of its life.

Nearly all dogs adapt in the course of about 40 lessons and ironically they then begin to react in an excited way when their owner appears with the face collar, just as they do when you produce a leash for a walk. It just requires time and perseverance. I have never met a person whose dog originally pulled and now walks nicely with a face collar who did not think it was worth the training effort.

Some dogs react badly when they are first introduced to a face collar, but it is worth persevering as they are very effective in controlling dogs that pull.

Reasons to Use
- Stops dogs pulling
- Few skills required by handler
- Calms many dogs down
- Often reduces aggressive displays

Introducing the Face Collar

First get your dog to sit while wearing a leash and collar. Then have several juicy tidbits (such as cheese or ham) on hand. Put on the face collar (the dog must be able to open its mouth with the muzzle fitted) and then reward the dog with a tidbit through the gaps in the collar. Leave it on the dog for a few minutes, remove it, and give another food reward. Your dog should now associate having the collar fitted with getting a reward.

This needs to be repeated three times a day for about ten minutes' duration for the next three days. The next step, on Day 4, is to attach the leash and fit the face collar to the dog, and walk the dog a few feet in the house or garden while rewarding the dog at short intervals. If your dog panics or attempts to rub its head on the floor (which is normal), distract it with the food and use your leash to make it sit. It's also useful to leave the muzzle on the dog in the house twice a day for about 10 to 15 minutes. When the dog begins to accept the muzzle without endless fuss, then you are beginning to reach normalization.

Most dogs resent the face collar at first, but quickly associate it with food reward and walks. Once you can walk your dog around the house or yard without adverse reaction, you are ready for the outdoors.

Chain Collars

Chain collars and slip collars tighten on a dog's neck when it pulls on the leash. They should only be used in very specific circumstances and under the guidance of a qualified trainer. They are not for general use, and are not featured as training aids in this book.

Electronic Spray Collars

These are collars that work by remote control at short distances. They emit a jet of foul-smelling but harmless citronella spray when the hand control unit is pressed. (It is not an electric shock collar.) I have used this successfully to teach recall in dogs that have learned to ignore or not respond to training methods, in order to get them back on command.

I do believe, however, that to use an electronic spray collar you need a good knowledge of how dogs learn. Training and timing are essential, and one should get help from a dog trainer to learn how to use the device correctly. It is not intended for, and neither should it be used, as a means of venting your frustration with a disobedient dog. Though the spray is innocuous, it can still greatly upset a few dogs when inappropriately used. The makers of the collar claim it can be used to train general obedience, but I feel this

would be a mistake. It's not a device to practice with at will — seek out expert help for the dog's benefit.

Reasons to Use
- Recall training
- Prevention of scavenging
- Stopping dogs pursuing livestock

A remote training collar emits a spray of strong-smelling vapor when its hand-held control unit is pressed. This startles the dog and interrupts it if it is not behaving.

TOYS, SPRAYS AND BEDS

Food, Toys and Other Playthings (puppy safe)

Certain well-made toys can be used in training. I use a toy called the Kong, which is a hollow rubber chewy receptacle in which food can be concealed. The dog enjoys chewing away at the toy and teasing out the morsels of food. It provides a pleasurable distraction on which the dog is happy to concentrate. It allows me to reward the dog for being attached to a hook and leash when I use this type of restraint in the Leadership Program. It immediately helps the dog to associate being tethered with a long-lasting reward as it tries to extract the food from the toy — instead of just focusing on the frustration of being restricted. The Kong can also be used as a retrieve toy.

There are some good quality, strong toys on the market. I generally use a solid rubber ball for the Retrieve. Tennis balls are unsafe because they can be squashed in

the dog's jaws only to resume their shape in its windpipe, causing serious harm. Rubber rings, rope toys and other such toys all allow you to interact playfully with a dog, helping to develop its mind and its sense of enjoyment of being with you.

Reasons to Use

- Recall
  - Active games (for mental stimulation)
  - For dogs that need extra stimulation
  - Can be assimilated into the dog training exercises described in this book

Deterrent Sprays (puppy safe)

Best Behavior or citronella are harmless, unpleasant smelling liquids that can be sprayed onto objects. They can help to stop your dog from chewing the leash or grabbing it as part of a game. The spray is particularly effective at dissuading puppies from using the leash as another chew toy, which is natural puppy behavior. Of course, the dog or pup takes its unrewarding cue from its action of chewing, not your previous action of spraying.

Reasons to Use

- Stops dogs, especially puppies, from mouthing the leash
  - Stops dogs and puppies from grabbing hands and arms if play-biting and mouthing are a problem

Dog Beds (puppy safe)

When they get a dog, the first thing many people do is to purchase a dog bed. It's a bit like giving a dog its own place in the house, its own personal space. Personally I don't use dog beds at all, as I don't want my dogs to feel that they have territorial possession of a bed or specific area in my home. However, most

There is a wide variety of strong, well-made toys on the market that can be incorporated successfully into many training exercises.

An effective countermeasure to use against dogs or puppies that grab and chew the leash or other items around the house is to spray it with a bitter-smelling spray. It is quite harmless, but the dog gets an unpleasant shock when it next starts to mouth the leash and no longer finds this particular game rewarding.

This boxer has grabbed the leash and is playing tug-of-war games with its owner. This isn't what you want when you start to practice heelwork.

people love buying dogs beds and I accept this as a personal preference. If you do have a dog bed, then it can be used as a special area for down and stay training. Once your dog naturally goes to its bed, you can link that with the training; it's also useful when you wish the dog to stay in its bed when circumstances dictate. Not all people like dogs pawing and begging for attention, and the bed can be a useful training aid to prevent this behavior. With repetition most dogs learn to go to their bed on command. I use the same techniques as for the hook restriction program (see page 28) to control the dog, or simply use a treat or two to lead the dog to the bed and to give it a reward for lying down when I want it to.

Reasons to Use

*   Helps at the beginning of stay training in the home
*   Once trained you can move the bed anywhere and the dog will generally go to it on command

As well as providing a place for dogs to rest and sleep, a bed can also be useful in training. For instance, it can be used in the early stages of teaching the Down/Stay exercise. You should regularly stand in the bed to demonstrate to the dog that you have the right to do so.

OTHER AIDS

Training Discs (puppy safe)

This relatively new training aid consists of five small metallic discs on a ring that clatter together noisily when they are thrown on the floor. If you can't find them at your local pet store, you can also use a chain or an old bunch of blunt keys to make a similar noise. Sound deterrents like this are useful in stopping misbehaving dogs in their tracks. I use the command **"No"** in conjunction with the discs. You need to precondition the dog to the discs beforehand to use them most effectively.

The psychology behind sound training is that the dog does not understand where the sound is coming

*Training discs can be used to stop a dog that is about to misbehave, such as by chewing someone's shoe. The dog comes to associate the unsettling noise of the discs striking the floor with the command **"No."***

Training discs clatter noisily when they hit the ground.

from and dogs are very suspicious of the unknown. If your dog is behaving badly, perhaps by stealing food, jumping up on you or barking excessively in the car or house, the discs will startle the dog when they are thrown down next to it. Here's how the discs work:

- The dog learns a sound and unpleasant association with whatever it's doing wrong
- It associates the sound with a command **"No"**

- Eventually it will respond instantly to the command **"No"** without the discs being used

One word of caution: use training discs with care with puppies, and only if other methods have been tried and exhausted first.

Reasons to Use

- To calm boisterous behavior
- To stop dogs jumping up
- To stop excessive barking in the car or at home

Whistles (puppy safe)

A good quality whistle is an essential when it comes to some of the methods of recall training (see Chapter 10). A whistle carries further than the human voice so it is especially useful when you have to attract the attention of a dog that has wandered out of earshot. I personally do not recommend clickers or clicker training.

Reason to Use

- Recall training

Food Rewards

I only use tidbits or food rewards in training and do not give my dogs any food treats at any other time, so they learn good manners and that harassing people won't get them food. Dogs that eat a healthy diet do not require additional tidbits or vitamin supplements. I recommend ham, cheese and chicken cut into very small chunks. Natural, fresh and far more appealing to dogs than manufactured processed pet snacks, these are easy to use and can be carried in a plastic container or bag tucked into a belt bag or your pocket. Use treats sparingly — I never use so many that they fill the dog up, especially in the case of smaller breeds and toy dogs. Labradors and German shepherds, on the other hand, can consume an awful lot of tidbits before they are sated.

Reasons to Use

- To reward the behavior that you are training
- To redirect the dog's attention and association back to your commands

Here we see two training aids in use at the same time. A whistle has been used to attract the attention of a dog that has wandered off some distance — possibly beyond the range of vocal recall — and a food tidbit is the dog's reward for coming back when called.

Chunks of ham, cheese and chicken make tasty food rewards.

A Clean Diet (puppy safe)

Though food (as opposed to treats) is not often referred to in training manuals, it can be a very potent influence over the way an animal behaves. Food is the vital ingredient of body maintenance and it affects behavior in dogs. Most dog foods, canned or dried, contain chemicals and additives that are apparently safe, although this remains a contentious issue, just as with foods designed for human consumption. I personally believe that dogs should be fed a natural diet that is guaranteed free of chemicals or additives. This removes the chance that any colorings or other chemicals present in the diet may affect behavior. I call this a "clean diet." Clean food does not require taste enhancement, added vitamins and the like. Good food by definition contains all the necessary requirements.

I have found a considerable change in dogs' behavior when they are fed a clean diet of fresh meat cooked with vegetables and rice. A dog I treated recently for noise phobia dramatically changed its behavior in less than two weeks by simply being fed a natural diet in conjunction with a behavioral correction course. Many hyperactive dogs change completely when their diet is changed to meat, vegetables and rice. You can test your dog by feeding it a natural food diet for a month and observing the results yourself. Remember that training a dog can be time-consuming, but training a dog that is detrimentally affected is much, much more difficult — so please consider diet carefully. A calm dog is an easier dog to train.

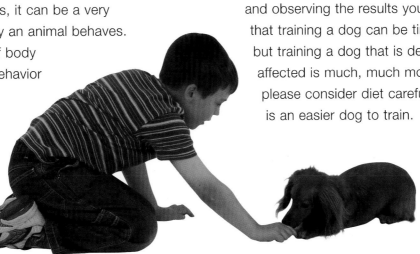

It takes time, but the rewards of owning a well-trained dog are certainly worth all the effort you put in.

CHAPTER SIX

Communication

Creating a New Language

If you watch dogs playing with one another in the park, it is clear that they are social animals who are able to communicate their moods and personalities to one another. They inherit this complex language from their wolf relations and, though much altered, the basic drives in the dog's mind still apply. How they approach one another is very important — their deportment, tail carriage and vocalization play a part in the dynamics of the meeting. A wagging tail does not necessarily signal good intentions — it depends on the circumstances and type of wag. Smell is crucial and dogs will sniff each other's genitalia

This dog's body language is deferential.

and other bodily areas to confirm status and identification. We miss out on all this information — mercifully so, some of you may think!

Though the dog is a pack animal like us, the dog's methods of communication differ — they rely chiefly on body language. But, perhaps surprisingly, despite our complex verbal language, we humans also use body language for up to 80 percent of our communication. So although our modes of spoken communication differ greatly, we have some common ground, a basic pattern of communication we can discover through trial and error. Dogs do have feelings and moods — they are not robots — but their emotional state is quite simple and child-like. This makes it difficult for us to relate to their moods when we are in a training situation.

In order to explain more efficient ways of training your dog, it's necessary to understand something of a dog's psychology. To get the best out of training, you may need to alter some of your preconceived ideas about dogs. Yes, they are incredible animals with which we have built up a unique relationship, but they do not, and cannot, think like us. They do not reason as we do and that fact alone can cause many problems in the owner-dog relationship. When a dog does something that you don't like, such as scratching a door or knocking a table over, it's no use admonishing it for an action that is done. Dogs, like little children, live for the moment. The past and future do not really come into the equation. When you have begun to appreciate their simple world, uncomplicated by rational thought, it becomes easier to begin dog training and to educate the dog who will hopefully spend its lifetime with you.

Because our pet dogs cannot behave as a natural pack would in the wild, they are forced to become part of the human family pack and to do their best to fit into our alien world. So they try to find their rank within the human family hierarchy. The higher the position they occupy, the more often than not conflict can occur. If they are taught by knowledgeable owners to know their position, which unreservedly is at the bottom of the human pack, they become more malleable and easier to train. That's good for all concerned.

The critical period for a puppy is between about 5 weeks and 12 weeks of age. A good deal of its temperament is formed at this early stage; the pup looks for instinctive responses from you and it will in turn try to communicate with you as it would with another dog. This is an ideal opportunity to teach what you want the pup to learn.

It is important to realize that dogs learn in a very black-and-white fashion, and mainly by association. So if an action like teaching the dog to sit produces a reward such as praise, food or touch, the dog will naturally wish to repeat that action. In the same way, if it smells food in a garbage can and knocks it over to get at the food, then that, too, is a rewarded response. Conversely, an unpleasant experience — perhaps the dog grabs some orange peel out of the trash and is upset by its acidic taste — produces an immediately unrewarding experience. The learned component of this experience is "Avoid the garbage and the orange."

Inherited Behavior

Depending on your dog's breed, it will inherit certain behavioral characteristics specific to the original breed type. This can cause training problems if you have not already taken such specific behavior into consideration. The hound breeds are bred to hunt and use their noses almost incessantly compared to, say, a Pekingese. So when training them in the outside world, it can be a struggle to get their attention. As puppies, toy breeds can be

Training depends on a vocabulary of commands.

so tiny that it is quite challenging to handle them, and you have to be fairly nimble physically to get down to their level for some of the training exercises.

The terrier breeds are certainly more excitable and triggered by anything that grabs their attention, while a Saint Bernard puppy seems to be about three seconds behind what is happening in the world. These breeds simply mature at different rates and have been bred for different jobs that require different reactions and temperaments. They all can be trained; we just need to be aware of these different factors while we are training them. All the shepherding breeds are much easier to obedience train but, if left to their own devices, they may use that innate intelligence to indulge in behavior that we don't want to encourage.

Dogs should occupy the bottom rung of the family pack — it makes them easier to live with and train.

HOW TO INFLUENCE BEHAVIOR

Tone of Voice

Different human vocal tones attract different reactions from a dog. The dog's reaction will vary depending on how high or low the tone is. It is therefore important to limit your commands to a single syllable like **"No"** rather than a confusing jumble of words like "You bad dog what have you done?" Command your dog in a crisp tone. Dogs can still understand the same command from adults and children who have obviously different voice patterns — the dog will adjust providing the trainer of whatever age is consistent in his or her vocal delivery.

"Good dog!" The use of a reward, like a food tidbit, is a potent way of getting a dog to repeat a behavior that you want to encourage.

Rewards

Dogs like rewards. Appreciation of what they have achieved is not a concern for them, but keeping in favor with pack members and especially the higher ranking ones is of importance. Dogs don't exactly see rewards as we do, but they can be a vital part of training that helps us to work with them. Understand that dogs will seek out behavior that is rewarding in itself. Rewards given by you, the leader, include attention, verbal praise, physical touch, tasty food, time in your company, retrieve games or any other action/response that gives the dog a feeling of being accepted by you. These are potent rewards for a dog.

In training, food is used often as a reward but be aware that it can be overused, and with many dogs this disrupts training. But if used in moderation, it can be very useful. Another powerful reward is play, which dogs love. They will often play on their own with toys, sticks or an old shoe, and so we use these items in dog training to further our ability to reward the dog. Dogs do enjoy life, and have the right personality to do so.

Unrewarding Experiences

I have described how dogs naturally seek out rewarding experiences and, not surprisingly, avoid unrewarding ones. That's not news to most people — we do the same. Punishment is the word often used for the unrewarding experiences that we use to help train dogs. It is not a term I like, for it has a vengeful connotation to me and is not appropriate for dealing with dogs. However, for ease of reference in this book we will use the term punishment for simplicity's sake. Dogs want to avoid unpleasantness. They don't like being hurt or upset or rejected from the pack. We

Dogs love play and they also enjoy the undivided attention of their pack leader. So a game like this is a powerful reward for training well.

can use such unrewarding experiences and manipulate the dog's senses and modify its behavior.

Direct punishment or an unrewarding experience can be many things. It may simply involve you ignoring the animal, rejecting its company. If the dog chews its leash, we can put a taste deterrent on it and that is truly unrewarding — it finds its own chewing actions unfruitful without our direct intervention. Most of all, like the wolf, we can use vocalized threats in our own way — which is simply the word **"No."** Holding a puppy firmly by the scruff of the neck and staring at it for a few seconds is quite a threat and works if you're skillful. Your high rank should allow you to act in this way without a problem. What you will not find in this book is any suggestion that you can hit your dog to discourage bad behavior — that is not recommended. We have other more effective ways of getting our way.

Here's an example that shows how the combination of reward and punishment can be applied in training. A dog surging ahead of you while simultaneously dragging you off your feet is upsetting. By using a leash and collar and snapping the dog down the leash when it pulls, your dog will find

The flipside of rewarding good behavior is to make bad behavior unrewarding. So if a dog surges ahead of you, a swift check down the leash will interrupt the dog's pulling.

the experience unpleasant. If skillfully implemented, the dog may associate pulling with the snap and stop pulling. Of course teaching the dog not to pull by rewarding it for not pulling is much easier and less confrontational. Better the carrot than the stick. Unfortunately, human nature means that when we lose our patience, we too often resort to punishing a dog and that, with few exceptions, slows down dog training.

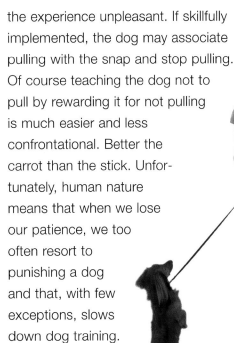

Don't ignore a dog that has trained well; you want to cement the link between a command, an action and a reward.

Timing

We have established that dogs will learn by associating any action that you are teaching it (in this case a training exercise) with a command backed up by a rewarding or unrewarding experience. How you go about this is crucial to how quickly the dog will learn. It all has to do with timing. Whether punishing or rewarding a dog, the reaction (the reward or punishment) must be delivered at the time of the action or at least within two seconds in order for the dog to begin to make a link between the two.

Most novice dog handlers find it hard at first to combine the full set of dog training skills — command, timing and praise — and consistently deliver them at the crucial moment. It's just a matter of practice; sometimes it's worth practicing your skills on your own before trying them out on your dog.

MAKING YOURSELF UNDERSTOOD

Motivation and Consistency

In a way rewards are motivation, but there are other ways of motivating a dog to want to be with you, to train and consequently to learn. The Leadership Program outlined in Chapter 3 is an excellent psychological way of manipulating your dog's instincts to pay attention at the times that you want. Linking the dog's innate desire to receive attention and have fun with you to training is good, but always make sure it's on your terms and not the dog's.

Make sure that everyone in the household uses the same commands and signals when training a family dog.

When the whole family is involved in a dog's education and training, everyone needs to be uniformly consistent. If you were learning a foreign language and you had four teachers who taught in very different ways, this would make learning more difficult. The family needs to agree beforehand on the commands to be used and training styles to be adopted. I have observed over many years how dogs sometimes respond to the commands of different family members according to the dog's perception of how high or low the people are in the family pecking order. Many women often lament to me that the dog pays much more attention to the husband than her. I find that in general dogs do pay more attention to the male voice, and a woman's more tolerant and forgiving nature can work against her. Dogs learn to obey when the training is clear and unambiguous and men often seem to act in a more direct fashion. Of course, many of the top trainers in the world are female — but if you watch them, you will see that they are always concise, clear and consistent.

Guilty or Not?

Do dogs experience guilt? At times it can appear that they do, but in reality their demeanor is more a signal of fear of your retribution. If an owner has been trying to catch his dog for an hour in the park and finally and angrily he eventually corners the dog, during his final approach the dog will often appear culpable and very deferential. We all too often assume that it knows why you are angry. Well, it doesn't. What the dog is aware of is that you are angry — it can interpret your body language more clearly than you think — and so it immediately takes up natural canine postures to pacify your apparent anger.

For the dog to be fearful, it must have experienced your anger before. If you punish the dog out of

Vocal commands must be crisp and hand signals clear and consistent. Inconsistency is the enemy of good training.

anger, it learns only the fact that you have punished it — not why. So bite your lip if things go wrong — I have done so on many occasions — and try to teach your dog the exercises in this book in a calm and positive frame of mind.

The Ignore — A Powerful Leadership Statement

The Alpha wolf ignores any pack member it chooses to and acknowledges whom it favors in the pack. It maintains much of its high status by the way it acknowledges the various pack members and when it does so. Pet dogs also respond exceedingly well to the amount we acknowledge their demands. If you genuinely ignore the unwanted behaviors your dog is trying to foist on you, they will normally stop. We usually fail because dogs are better at being consistently and repetitively manipulative than we are at ignoring their remonstrations. Dogs have incredible patience that must stem from their natural hunting behavior.

Many dogs bark when they want our attention simply because they have learned that this works. Barking is definitely not wolf behavior, but one of the adaptations of the domestic dog. If you can, ignore the barking (and ignoring means avoiding eye contact too). In all but exceptional cases, the barking stops. Conversely, acknowledging your dog's good behavior — such as when it comes, sits or lies down on command — with pats and vocal praise encourages the dog to repeat these exercises. So the Ignore is a powerful statement and you the leader need to use it effectively. Be a wolf.

I have found it instructive to observe owners when they visit my center for dog behavior problems. When told to ignore their dog for ten minutes, nine out of ten of them actually acknowledge their dog many times. But they are not aware of this until one of my trainers points out the subtle manner in which they have acknowledged the dog — often through a slight inclination of the head in the dog's direction when it whimpers, barks or nudges them. It's the dogs who are the clever ones.

Behavior Alteration and Communication Skills — Review

- The critical periods for temperament formation in dogs is between 5 and 12 weeks of age

- Inherited behavior is fixed like other breed traits, e.g., temperament, color, size, shape

- Develop your "toneology" — the ability to use your voice effectively in training

- Rewards should be given at the time of learning a command or within two seconds of it

- Punishment should be given at the time of learning a command or within two seconds of it

- Timing is the owner's ability to produce a learning link between what is being taught and a reward being given

- Consistency is a key to training — the trainer should repeat a set of commands and actions in the same way each time

- Guilt is a human concept, not a canine one

- The Ignore is a powerful learning tool that dogs are able to understand

HAND SIGNALS

Hand Signals

Dogs are very observant and can spot movement very acutely, especially at a distance. Close up they have poor eyesight compared to us. If you wish to add hand signals to complement your training commands, then this can be done as soon as your dog begins to follow your verbal commands consistently. Hand signals are just another link in the chain, like the whistle. Hand signals are very useful when the dog is at some distance from you.

I say hand signals, but dogs are masters of inter-preting body language and so take far more from your physical training style than just the movements of your arm and hand. Take the situation when you train a dog to lie down using food as a motivator. The food is taken from just in front of the dog's nose down to the floor for the dog to follow. As you execute this action simultaneously with the command **"Down,"** your hand, arm and part of your body articulates with that whole movement. Dogs notice this and the whole body movement becomes the signal in time. If your dog is a small breed, you may have to bend down fully before beginning the action of lowering the food down, so the dog takes its cue from you bending down first. The subtleties of a person's body actions are readily apparent to most dogs.

Here are some pictures of the signals used in the basics of dog training so that you will understand the essential "vocabulary" needed to begin the training program.

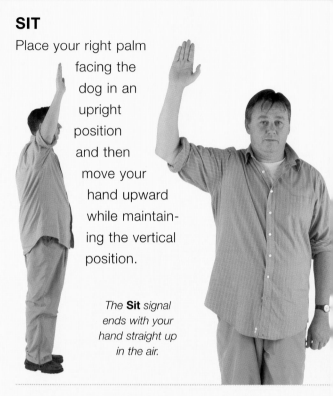

SIT
Place your right palm facing the dog in an upright position and then move your hand upward while maintaining the vertical position.

*The **Sit** signal ends with your hand straight up in the air.*

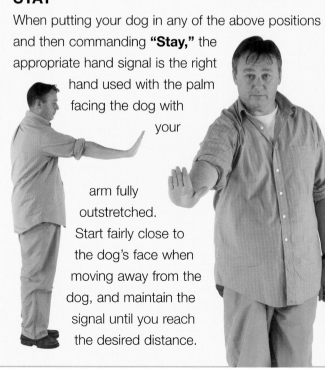

STAY
When putting your dog in any of the above positions and then commanding **"Stay,"** the appropriate hand signal is the right hand used with the palm facing the dog with your arm fully outstretched. Start fairly close to the dog's face when moving away from the dog, and maintain the signal until you reach the desired distance.

STAND

Using your right hand, move your arm out from your hip to the right slightly diagonally.

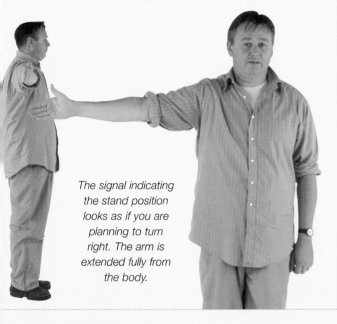

The signal indicating the stand position looks as if you are planning to turn right. The arm is extended fully from the body.

DOWN

For the down position, your palm should be facing the ground level with your chest, with your arm outstretched in front of you. Then make a clear downward movement to below your waist.

COME (Recall)

First it is necessary to get your dog's attention; once it is looking at you, extend your arm diagonally down towards the ground and bring your palm in towards your chest in a "gathering in" motion. Another option is to stretch out both arms with palms facing the dog at about waist height. As soon as you have the dog's attention, lower your bodily position so that you become more appealing to run to. The hands are then taken from the outstretched position down to about knee level and brought together in one clear movement.

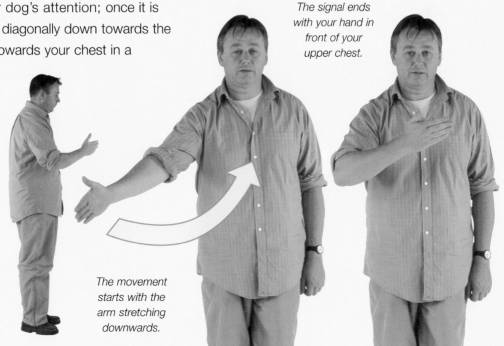

The signal ends with your hand in front of your upper chest.

The movement starts with the arm stretching downwards.

THE
TRAINING
PROGRAM

CHAPTER SEVEN

The 21-Day Training Plan

To help your dog reach a good basic standard of obedience I have developed a general 21-day training program. Try to apply the plan bearing in mind your dog's breed type, age and individual circumstances. If your dog is reasonably well behaved but just needs to learn basic dog training, then you should no doubt reach the desired standard in 21 days. For people who are training very young puppies the course is fine, but continuation training is essential. A little extra effort will be needed with older dogs that are badly behaved and who have perhaps been through a number of training courses, but you should still reach a good basic standard of obedience.

Remember that before you start the training program, you should place your dog on the Leadership Program (see Chapter 3) for at least a week. This will adjust your dog's attitude and help to concentrate its mind on you as the new full-time leader of the pack.

Sit

Stand

Down

Stay

Come

COMMANDS USED	EXERCISE	COMMANDS USED	EXERCISE
"Heel"	To walk at your side	"Come"	Recall
"Sit"	The Sit position	"In"	Dog enters car
"Stand"	The Stand position	"Come"	Dog exits car
"Down"	The Down position	"Fetch"	Dog retrieves toy
"Stay"	To stay in the Sit, Stand and Down positions	"Good dog"	Verbal praise
"Free"	The release command	"No"	Expression of admonishment

TRAINING PROGRAM

Divide each day into three lessons and train for approximately 15 minutes per lesson. The exercises are summarized below. Puppies require only about five minutes training per lesson. If you wish to train four or five times a day, that's fine; it will speed up training. If your dog still seems interested and keen at the end of the lesson, you can train for a little longer, but never to the point where the dog begins to become bored. Remember to play a fun game with your dog at the end of the lesson — it really does help to teach the dog to look forward to its training.

WEEK 1

Heel Walk in the heel position — in squares, figure eights around trees, along roads and in your yard.
Sit position 3 times per lesson.
Stand position 3 times per lesson.
Down position 3 times per lesson.
Stay on a leash 3 times per lesson.
Recall 1 to 5 times in your yard and house.
Retrieve at lesson end and enjoy a fun game.

WEEK 2

Heel Walk in the heel position — in and around the house, along the street, in the park.
At the heel **Sit** position 5 times.
At the heel **Stand** position 5 times.
At the heel **Down** position 5 times.
Down/Stay drop the leash and walk away; face your dog 3 times for a duration of up to two minutes.
Sit/Stay drop the leash and walk away; face your dog 3 times for a duration of up to one minute.
Stand/Stay drop the leash and walk away; face your dog 3 times for a duration of up to 30 seconds.
Recall 5 times. Practice in a quiet area in the yard or park.

WEEK 3

Heel Walk in the heel position — in and around the house, along the street, in the park
At the heel **Sit** position 5 times.
At the heel **Stand** position 5 times.
At the heel **Down** position 5 times.
Down/Stay drop the leash and walk away; face your dog 3 times for a duration of up to three minutes.
Sit/Stay drop the leash and walk away; face your dog 3 times for a duration of up to two minutes.
Stand/Stay drop the leash and walk away; face your dog 3 times for a duration of up to one minute.
Recall as many times as practicable. Practice in a quiet area.

Note: Do not preface each command with your dog's name – it's just confusing, and you want clarity. Always call the dog's name before a recall command, but otherwise only use it when you need to get its attention for any reason.

EXERCISE SUMMARY

Exercise Summary

The following summary is intended as a handy quick-reference guide when you need to quickly check something. Full descriptions of how to accomplish the various disciplines, as well as photographs showing training in progress, will be found in the appropriate chapters that follow. The commands listed below should be used in conjunction with the reward you have found best for your dog.

HEEL: To begin, your dog should be on your left side, and the leash held in your right hand only. Walk off, simultaneously giving the command **"Heel."** If the dog forges ahead, give the command **"Heel."** Once the dog is back, praise it — **"Good dog"** — with a soft, gentle voice. If your dog lags behind, under no circumstances snap the leash, just use praise to encourage it back to your side.

DOWN position: First place your dog in the sit position, then gently pull down toward the ground with a shortened leash and simultaneously command **"Down."**

STAY positions: Place your dog in the sit position, extend the leash to its full length, then take a few steps ahead to your right. Command the dog to **"Stay"** before you leave. If your dog stays, return to its side and praise it. Don't be too effusive with praise on the return as this may excite the dog and cause it to move prematurely. The same discipline can be carried out in the stand and down positions.

SIT position: Walk off with your dog in the heel position and come to an abrupt halt. Pull the leash upward with your right hand, command **"Sit,"** then praise the dog.

STAND position: Again, walk off with the dog and come to a gentle halt. The leash is in your right hand, so use your left hand to touch the dog's tummy, in conjunction with the command **"Stand."** Praise the dog.

RECALL: In the garden or park use the appropriate equipment with the whistle, line, toys and food when required.

FREE: When the training lesson is completed, use the command **"Free"** to signal that formal training is over, and perhaps play a short game with your dog.

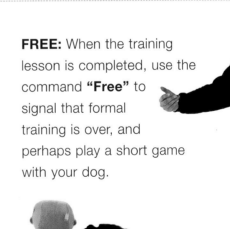

GENERAL ADVICE

Advice Before You Start

Begin your training in the yard, a quiet part of the house or another calm place with no distractions. Continue to practice there for the first lessons, until you have reached a standard where your dog responds to your commands. If the dog is progressing well, you can then ask family members to distract the dog mildly, which will allow you to reinforce your commands and maintain the dog's focus on training despite what's going on around it.

Once your dog understands the basics of each command, the next stage is to practice all of the exercises in different training locations, e.g., the street, park or other public places. Note: when near a road or on a sidewalk, all exercises must be carried out on a leash — **no exceptions.**

At first your dog will be distracted; this is normal, but now you have to work harder. The dog may find the distractions more interesting than you or what you are trying to teach it. Of course, this will depend also on what the dog has already learned to date, and how much it is used to getting its own way. This is a time when a number of owners give up, because their dog appears to be regressing, but this is not so! The dog does not forget what you have taught it, but in these situations instantly comes to expect either your positive enforcement of the obedience or lack of it. Your dog has to be obedient in all circumstances so do not give up — **keep going!** Within a few days the dog will respond to your commands.

When training in a public place, other dogs may run to you and your dog. Their intentions may be friendly, or their owners may have little or no control over them. Under these circumstances, especially in the first few weeks of training, it is best to heel your dog off briskly to another area. Your dog cannot be expected to learn while other dogs are making a nuisance of themselves.

When heeling your dog down a street, it is natural for your dog to be curious when other dogs pass by. Don't stop — just carry on walking, praising your dog back to your side. Alternatively, you can snap the leash on your dog if it stubbornly pulls towards them. Your dog must not learn that every time it sees a dog in the street or park it means it can assume the leadership role. You may wish your dog to play and socialize with other dogs when you choose. This is perfectly acceptable, as long as your dog is under **obedient** control.

When you have reached a stage where you feel you have control of your dog by command only, then by all means relax the rules a little. Allow your dog free playtime with other dogs that will allow it to socialize and develop good, sound canine traits.

However, this should not reach the stage where your dog pursues every dog in sight as a matter of course. Dogs that chase every other dog in the park, for whatever reason, are a nuisance. Your dog should be more interested in you as a trainer and pack leader, and to achieve this focus, play ball or another game and call the dog to you several times on each walk, giving lots of praise when it is due. Don't leave recall until home time arrives, as your dog may start to associate the recall command with being taken home, signaling the end of its enjoyment.

TRAINING TIPS

1. Before you begin training your dog, be sure you fully understand the exercise you are about to teach. Do not attempt any exercise if you are in doubt. If this is the case, refer to the book again.

2. The motivation for your dog to learn is praise (and other rewards) delivered in a pleasant tone of voice. Remember this throughout the training program. Very few dogs need physical correction — rely on patience and repetitive training, with a play period at the end.

3. Few dogs deliberately disobey you, but if they do, correct the way you use your voice, make it firmer. If your dog is having a bad day, try standing still; at least that stops your dog getting its own way. Remember, if the dog appears to be making mistakes, the fault usually lies with the trainer not communicating their message clearly enough.

4. When training, your dog may begin to lose interest. If that's the case, introduce an exercise it likes, praise the dog, finish training, play a short game, then begin again later on in the day.

5. When teaching the recall on a long line in a public place, do not allow your dog to play with other dogs, as the line may get tangled in their feet. If too many dogs arrive, call your dog to you, praise it, then put it on its normal leash and walk off.

6. You should be aware that different breeds, born with different working instincts, progress in training at different rates.

7. Rescue dogs or dogs that have learned many bad habits and are determined to do what they want can still be trained, but it can be harder. That's the challenge. It's basically a case of your skills and patience gradually redirecting the dog's behavior to what you want. These dogs always benefit from the Leadership Program being implemented immediately.

CHAPTER EIGHT

Heelwork

Dogs that pull are a nuisance — especially if the dog is large and strong. Being dragged along can be a serious problem and is certainly an unpleasant experience. Dogs that drag owners usually don't get walked as often as dogs that are obedient and are a pleasure to walk. Only certain members of the family are capable of controlling some dogs by virtue of their strength, and this can have a detrimental effect on the lifestyle of many dogs — not the ideal situation. Other owners practice complicated schemes to get around the problem by conveying the dog from front door to park gate in the car and then letting the dog burst out of the vehicle at full speed while the owner desperately tries to unclip the leash from its collar before their fingers are dislocated.

Of course, even the worst canine pullers in the world are not trying to upset you personally. They are completely unaware of your plight. Your pleading or angry objections are just sounds playing in the background of a carefree run. Yet the majority of dogs I see for a problem behavior like excessive pulling have already attended a dog training course. This has been unhelpful for a number of reasons. Many instructors use ineffective methods that do not stem pulling but

Well-trained dogs are a pleasure to walk.

do often exhaust the handler to the point of giving up. The training program I use is effective, however, as it starts teaching you about canine communication.

Commands – A New Language

To the casual observer, an owner and a dog with pulling problems is an unusual sight. It's a bit like someone who speaks English trying to communicate with a foreigner simply by talking louder. Dog owners often resort to the same tactic, but all the dog learns is that you can talk and yell at different volumes.

I use certain simple commands for simplicity and consistency — you may use your own commands if that suits you — but they must be short, preferably just a single syllable. Praise should be given in a very soft tone of voice (whispering is ideal, like we do with babies) so that your dog can distinguish commands from praise. Equally, the dog should understand the word **"No"** and this should be delivered in a sharp, commanding, crisp tone. Don't constantly keep saying **"Good dog,"** interrupted only by **"Heel," "Sit"** and so on. This becomes a drone and it is very difficult for your dog to learn what you want. Deliver your command **"Heel,"** then walk off. If the dog remains by your side, whisper **"Good dog."** If after a few strides it begins to wander ahead, command **"Heel"** firmly, tap your side simultaneously and, if the dog returns, give soft verbal praise. The silences in between allow your dog to take note of the commands and reward as distinct sounds and associate them with your particular actions or positions. In other words, decide what commands you will use before beginning training, and keep them consistent.

BEGINNING HEEL TRAINING

COMMAND
"HEEL"

START : 1
For teaching heelwork, I recommend that the dog should be positioned on your left side and the leash held in your right hand. This leaves the left hand free to tap your side to encourage the dog to heel.

2
*When you are ready to begin training, deliver your **"Heel"** command in a firm tone of voice and walk off to the front.*

3
*Initially the dog may surge well ahead of you. If that's the case, command **"Heel"** again and when the dog returns to your side, praise it in a gentle tone.*

COMMAND
"HEEL"

4
Use your free left hand to tap your side to let the dog know where you want it to position itself.

COMMAND
"HEEL"

5
*Praise your dog at the end of the exercise – say **"good dog."***

***Above:** It's no fun walking a dog that consistently pulls, and when you are dealing with an animal as big as this, it is exhausting and potentially dangerous. If you own a dog, it really is vital that you should train it to walk obediently at your heel.*

EARLY TRAINING

For control, make sure you have the correct leash and collar. You may wonder why I position the dog on my left, but hold the leash in my right hand. This is because it leaves the left hand nearest the dog as a working tool. The right hand controls the leash.

I always teach my dogs to walk on my left and at my heel. It's not essential that all dogs walk in this position, but I recommend it as it promotes continuity and frees my hands to assist in training. In my view it helps if a dog knows consistently which side it's walked on. However, whether your dog walks 1 m (3 ft.) ahead of you or not is only important if you feel that it is. That's why some dogs on a long leash can walk slightly ahead of their owner without wanting to pull any further. Of course, this is not ideal in the city where you have to cope with busy pedestrian traffic. The best position then is to have your dog at your left side with its head about level with your body. This is known as the Heel. It enables you to turn in any direction without tripping over the dog.

Begin your heel training in the backyard, a quiet part of the house or any other quiet place where you will not be bothered by distractions. Continue to practice there for the first few weeks, until you have reached a standard whereby the dog responds consistently to your Heel and Sit commands.

Heel Training for Puppies

When you train a puppy on a leash and collar, it's obvious that these little creatures are incredibly malleable and can learn to walk next to you in a matter of weeks providing there is enough motivation in your handling. While this chapter is mostly concerned with dogs that pull, it is useful to go over some basic training information for puppies because that's the ideal age to train a dog. I train from six weeks of age. Other people may think that's too young for training but in my professional capacity I have only seen positive results when training from this age. I begin training in the house, hallway, kitchen and yard. Each session lasts just a few minutes.

A puppy has no idea what you want, or why pulling is not part of walking on a leash and collar. Why should it? There is no place in wolf evolution for a collar and leash, nor walking at our pedestrian pace, which is slower than the dog's natural gait. However, once a puppy has been accustomed to the collar and leash in the home, we can tentatively begin heel training.

When heel training, I always motivate the dog by some action which gives me its attention and then give it a corresponding reward when it acts correctly. This gives the puppy pleasure. Using a tidbit and/or a squeaky toy, I walk off giving the command **"Heel."** When the puppy surges ahead of me, I turn to the right, simultaneously bending down with an outstretched left hand which is either holding a squeaky toy or offering a (tiny) tasty treat. As the puppy takes this cue and follows my hand, I command **"Heel"** and give the tidbit or let the puppy mouth the toy. After repeating this action ten or more times, I throw the toy for the puppy to make a little game and finish. I begin a new lesson later. The puppy has now begun to pay attention, to learn the command **"Heel,"** and has found that being by my side at all times brings fun and rewards.

Puppies will often panic when they are first connected to a leash and collar so it imperative that you allow the puppy to get used to the leash and collar

before any training begins. You can do this by simply allowing the pup to drag the leash around while in your company. You can also hold the leash and reward the pup with some tidbits. If at any stage the puppy lunges ahead and begins to panic when the leash tightens, drop the leash immediately as this eliminates the tension and feeling of restriction. As soon as the puppy relaxes, pick up the leash again and wander around the room. Repeated sufficiently often, this familiarizes the pup to the leash and collar without a problem.

START : 1
It is also possible to teach an older puppy heelwork off the leash.

COMMAND
"HEEL"

2
Command "Heel" as the puppy walks alongside you.

TRAINING OFF THE LEASH

3
If the puppy starts to wander off line or begins to lose concentration, turn to the right and at the same time bend down and offer the tidbit or treat that's in your fingers.

PUPPY TRAINING ON THE LEASH

In the early stages of training a puppy to walk to heel, use a food tidbit or a squeaky toy to give the puppy a tangible reward to enjoy when it obeys your commands. The tidbit also gives the exercise a visual focus so that the puppy's attention is directed at you. While I recommend training with the leash in the right hand, it's not a sin to relax the rules sometimes and do what feels comfortable.

4
As the puppy takes the cue, command "Heel" again to link the verbal signal to the action.

COMMAND
"HEEL"

COMMAND
"HEEL"

5
Finish off with praise and a little game. It keeps a sense of fun.

COMMAND
"HEEL"

HEELWORK BASICS

Heel Turns

From puppies, let's turn our attention to adult dogs and the basics of heel training that they must learn. The main purpose of teaching a dog to walk comfortably by your side is to enable the two of you to negotiate sidewalks and streets and to weave your way through crowds of pedestrians who do not necessarily take any notice of your dog and its position.

Therefore it's important that your dog should learn to stick close by your left side so that wherever you walk it will be nearby. To help teach the dog this work we use a number of bodily techniques known collectively as the heel turns. In simple terms: **we use visual, verbal and physical communication to make our intentions clear to the dog.** We use our arms, legs and body movements to nudge, guide and maneuver the dog to respond to our directions and to stop it pulling on the leash ahead or tripping us up by moving across our path.

The idea is to be like two ballroom dancers keeping their eyes on one another's movements. The dog must learn to keep an eye on its handler — you. When you walk along chatting with a friend, you instinctively keep close as you move through hordes of other pedestrians. That skill probably took us years to learn from childhood and we have a concept of what we are doing and what we want to do. The dog has no such notion and is being asked to learn this technique in a very short period of time relative to its human counterparts.

Heel — Walking Forward

Begin with your dog sitting on your left side. Your right hand holds the leash with a slight loop across to the dog's collar. If your leash is 2 m (6 ft.) long, then loop it once to shorten it. Your left hand only comes into play if the dog begins to surge ahead — otherwise it's free. This may seem odd at first to the beginner. When ready, walk off tapping your side with your left hand and command **"Heel."** If the dog surges or begins to get ahead of you, command **"Heel"** again, tap your left thigh and praise the dog when it returns to your side.

If you're ignored, take the leash in both hands and snap it sharply once, releasing it immediately. The snap — which should take only a fraction of a second — sends a pulse of energy down the leash to the dog's neck and serves as a way of gathering its attention. **Never drag the dog back.** As the dog is momentarily halted by the snap, command **"Heel"** again and encourage the dog in an excited tone to return to your side. Use lots of praise and touch rewards upon its return. If the dog really pulls ahead hard, stop momentarily, command **"Sit,"**

SNAP THE LEASH

4
The snap should be swift and quickly released.

5
Practice makes perfect – and a happy dog and owner.

pause and begin again. Don't forget that the turn techniques described next also teach the dog not to surge ahead. When all the turns are combined on a walk, your dog learns that it must pay attention if it is to see where you are walking because it is unable to predict your sudden changes of direction. For your dog not to be caught unaware, it has to be positioned at your heel to see you all the time. That's the point of the training.

THE LEASH SNAP

START : 1

To begin heelwork training have the dog positioned on your left, walk off, tap your left side and command ***"Heel."***

2

If the dog starts to pull ahead, command ***"Heel"*** *again, and tap your side.*

COMMAND
"HEEL"

COMMAND
"HEEL"

CIRCUIT TRAINING

This shows how getting the message over to a dog which is learning heelwork relies on a combination of repeated verbal commands, physical taps of the hand against the leg and persuasive body language on the part of the handler. A 2 m (6 ft.) leash is used because it can be shortened for heelwork and lengthened for the initial stay exercises.

3

On occasion the dog will not respond correctly to your command and keeps pulling. In that case you can take the leash in both hands and administer a sharp snap with it.

COMMAND
"HEEL"

COMMAND
"HEEL"

COMMAND
"HEEL"

When the exercise goes well, both handler and dog move as a team, each aware of and responsive to the other.

COMMAND
"HEEL"

START

LEFT TURNS

The Left Turn (puppy safe)

Walking off in a straight line as described above, turn left across your dog's front. Pivoting on your left foot, use your right knee to emphasize the turn left. Your right hand naturally holds the leash; simultaneously use your left hand to take hold of the leash about halfway along its length to add control and pull it into your waist. When you have turned left, use your right hand to take up the slack leash. Your left hand is now free for petting, touching or tapping your side for encouragement as the dog stays close by your side. Dogs that don't pay attention often get a surprise at this sharp left turn and quickly learn to pay attention to what you are doing rather than what they are interested in, like scents. A bit of amateur dramatics can also help — act excited and use quick movements. This behavior combined with an animated tone of voice can and do encourage a reticent dog to turn quickly and walk or trot toward you as you head off in the new direction. It's also fun.

Making Turns with a Smaller Dog

When practicing turns with medium and large-sized dogs, you will find that you can use your knee to emphasize the movement you are making in order to help coax the dog into altering direction with you. With smaller dogs this is not possible as they carry their heads too close to the ground for the handler's knee to come into play.

So when training with small dogs you have to rely more on your own body language, leg tapping and excited verbal praise to keep the dog moving in parallel with you. With smaller dogs, you may also use your right foot to nudge the dog to a semi-halt as you pivot. Try to maintain the dog's interest by acting in a lively manner.

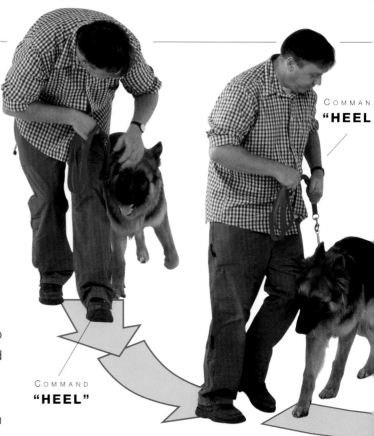

COMMAND
"HEEL"

COMMAND
"HEEL"

PRAISE
"GOOD DOG"

START : 1
Small dogs cannot be guided by the handler's knee.

2
Instead use verbal praise and taps of your leg to help keep the dog on track.

COMMAND
"HEEL"

START : 1

As you make the turn to the left, pivot on your left leg while raising the right knee high in an exaggerated manner and using it to direct the dog's head toward your new direction of travel.

2

Once the dog has responded and is moving off in the desired direction, you can use your free left hand to give the dog a brief pat or to tap your knee to encourage it to keep close to your heel.

PRAISE
"GOOD DOG"

Make your movements purposeful and decisive.

COMMAND
"HEEL"

2

As you make the pivoting movement, the dog will come to a semi-halt for a moment.

START : 1

For the left about turn, you spin fully around.

The Left About Turn (puppy safe)

This begins like the left turn but instead of turning left at a 90-degree angle, you actually pivot fully back so that you are facing in the opposite direction. Command **"Heel"** as you begin the turn. This takes a little practice, but once mastered it really does help to teach your dog not to pull and to pay attention to you. It is quite a dramatic full turn. With small dogs, simply use your right foot to nudge your dog to a semi-halt as you pivot. As you walk off again in a straight line, give lots of dramatic praise for the dog being back at your side. With larger dogs your right knee may nudge/guide the dog to a semi-halt as you turn back on it.

RIGHT TURNS

The Right Turn (puppy safe)

Walking off as above in a straight line, turn sharp right, pivoting on your left foot and striding out with your right leg. Lower your body and, again, your left hand joins your right on the leash, but this time you drop your hands low to give your dog more leash length as you turn right. Remember it will be surging straight ahead unaware at first of your turn to the right. If the dog sees your turn and begins to turn also, praise it enthusiastically as it returns to your left side. Once you are upright again and walking straight, let go of the leash with your left hand. Remember to keep the leash loose, but not too long, otherwise you cannot quickly control the dog if it surges ahead again. Dogs that pay attention are not often surprised by this sharp right turn and learn to be watchful of your movements. Use an excited tone of praise to encourage your dog back to your left side — this really helps the dog to concentrate on you. Once walking normally, stop talking and praise the dog occasionally for still being by your side.

The Right About Turn (puppy safe)

The right about turn also begins like the right turn, but you make a full 180-degree turn back along the route that you have just walked along. In other words, if the dog is not paying attention it will now be walking in one direction while you are walking in the opposite one. However, the leash connects you both and soon makes your intentions clear. As you execute the turn, command **"Heel"** to give the dog the opportunity to turn with you and to receive your praise. Remember to give dramatic praise if the dog begins to turn and return to your side.

Food rewards are helpful to encourage a dog to turn with you and to keep its attention focused on your movements.

Training Tips

• With all the turns command **"Heel"** as you turn; this alerts the dog that you are about to change direction.

• Praise the dog telling it that it is **"good"** in a whisper if it keeps by your side during the turn. Use food or a toy as an added attraction.

• If you need to snap the leash, make it short and sharp, more of an inconvenience to the dog surging ahead. **Never drag the dog to you at any time.**

• If you are using food as a reward, make sure it's in your left pocket or in a belt bag so that it's easily accessible to give as you make a turn.

• You can also use a toy in the same way as food to reward and encourage a dog to make a turn.

• Always use touch to gain your dog's attention and always use verbal praise when it performs obediently.

MAKING A RIGHT TURN

To make a right turn you pivot on your left foot. This may catch the dog by surprise as you are turning away from its direction of travel, so bend lower as you swing around and drop your hands to give the dog a bit more leash length through the turn.

START : 1
Take up the slack if using a long leash.

PRAISE
"GOOD DOG"

COMMAND
"HEEL"

MAKING A RIGHT ABOUT TURN

PRAISE
"GOOD DOG"

COMMAND
"HEEL"

2
For an about turn you pivot sharply on one leg and walk off in the opposite direction.

4
As the dog makes the full 180° turn with you, reward it with an encouraging word of praise.

3
This German shepherd is paying attention and has spotted that its owner is turning.

HEELWORK PRACTICE

3
Perfect! Owner and dog are now walking along in an ideal heel position.

2
Instead you should pat your side and use praise to encourage it to catch up.

P R A I S E
"GOOD DOG"

START : 1
If your dog lags behind you when practicing heelwork, resist the temptation of hauling it physically back to your side.

Once you have mastered all the turns, preferably in your yard or house first, the dog will quickly start to appreciate the fun of training and be happy to concentrate on your actions. You are now leading. The dog is led, but also enjoys learning to walk on a loose leash by your left side.

Heel Training with Dogs

The techniques described above are the first stage in teaching older dogs to heel. The next stage is to practice the heel exercises in different training locations as well as on the sidewalk, and in the park and other public places. At first your dog will be distracted; this is normal, but now you have to work harder. The dog may find everything going on around it much more interesting than you or the training exercises. Don't despair and don't give up — your dog may appear to be regressing, but this is not really the case. You just have to recapture its attention.

When heeling your dog down a street, it is natural when other dogs pass by for your dog to be inquisitive. **Don't be tempted to stop** — carry on walking, praising your dog as it comes back to your side. It often helps to offer a treat as a greater distraction than the passing dog. Equally, you can snap the leash on

an adult dog if it insists on pulling in their direction. But **never do this with a puppy.** Sometimes I begin to run for few feet, and most dogs find this exciting and prefer to follow rather than pulling toward the other dog. Again, dramatics can help. Your dog must not come to think that every time it sees another dog in the street or park, it no longer has to listen to you. Obviously, you might want your dog to play and socialize with other dogs when you think it's right. This is perfectly acceptable, as long as your dog is under control. If you believe that by stopping and allowing your dog to exchange sniffs with the passing dog, this will satisfy its curiosity and reduce the problem, you are mistaken. It will just teach your dog that a new dog approaching means **"Stop."**

I use another technique with adult dogs. If the dog really surges ahead, I stop, tell the dog to **"Sit"** and do not move again until it calms down. I have stopped a hundred times with one dog on a long stretch of road until this particular Labrador got the message that if you pull, I stop. Patience is obviously required, and you may need to persist over many weeks of training. If your dog lags behind you, under no circumstances pull it; just use praise to encourage it back to your side.

Pay Attention

Teaching your dog to pay attention to you is the critical factor that the dog has to learn, and this means that you have to learn ways of making yourself attractive to your dog when it is being walked. This is teamwork — you and your dog have to turn into a double act, watching each other all the time. If you have a dog that has already learned to pull and/or has started to ignore you, you will have to go back to square one. This means making sure that the dog has been on the Leadership Program described in Chapter 3 for at least a week. The dog will be more ready to listen, and will be prepared to give you its attention linked to the command and training you want to teach.

House Training Plan

Strange as it may seem, it's a good idea to begin leash training in the house. Most dogs react excitedly when the leash is produced so use that conditioned enthusiasm for indoor training. Clip the leash onto the collar but simply walk around the house. If your dog likes treats, use bits of cheese or ham as rewards. Your dog is on your left and the leash is in your right hand. The treats will be given with the left hand, so perhaps wear a coat with baggy pockets for easy access to the treats in the left pocket. Command **"Heel"** and walk off. When you turn left, right, left about or right about, command **"Heel."** If your dog stays near your side, offer a treat. If it surges ahead, about turn and simultaneously bend low as illustrated in the photograph and offer the treat near the dog's nose. Draw the dog to you as it follows the treat back to your left side. Give the treat, say **"Heel"** and praise with a **"Good dog!"** Be dramatic! Over-the-top performances attract dogs more than monotonous training styles. Of course, if you have a highstrung dog that tends to get overexcited, you should tone down the drama.

START : 1
You can practice leash and heelwork training simply by walking around your house and executing turns with the dog at your side.

COMMAND
"HEEL"

START

3
When performing circuits like this, vary your left and right turns.

TRAINING AT HOME

2
Use your left hand to give treats as rewards.

COMMAND
"HEEL"

COMMAND
"HEEL"

BACKYARD TRAINING

Backyard Training Plan (puppy safe)

If you have a backyard, perform the same routines you did indoors outside, but now include a figure-eight pattern into the heel turns. Your main concern is to make sure that the dog's attention is focused on you, so remember to keep tapping your left side, and offer a few excited words of encouragement as the dog nears the proper heel position. In other words, a positive response from you should only occur when the dog is approaching or at your side.

In larger rooms or bigger yards if your dog seems to be losing interest or wishes to pull toward an enticing scent, break into a trot or run. This ignites many a dog's interest, as movement for dogs is intrinsically exciting. Run for 5 m (15 ft.) or so and then drop back to a walk again once the dog has come by your side. If the dog begins to wander off to the left, you should suddenly turn sharp right, letting the leash out and commanding **"Heel"** as you turn. If the dog does not turn when you do, a sharp tug or snap on the leash to get its attention is helpful, but never drag the dog. Remember the leash snap is intended to gain the dog's attention. As the dog notices that you have changed direction and hears your command, it will follow. As it does so, excitedly praise the dog back to your left side. A treat may then be offered. You can then continue on your way.

As you practice this training routine and repeat it many times, your dog learns that by keeping by your side it gets a touch reward, a verbal reward and sometimes a food reward. It begins to associate the command **"Heel"** with being by your side. It also learns that when it loses concentration of where you are, you may suddenly turn and a snap will come down the leash, signaling your new direction. At the end of each lesson return to the house, unclip the dog and relax.

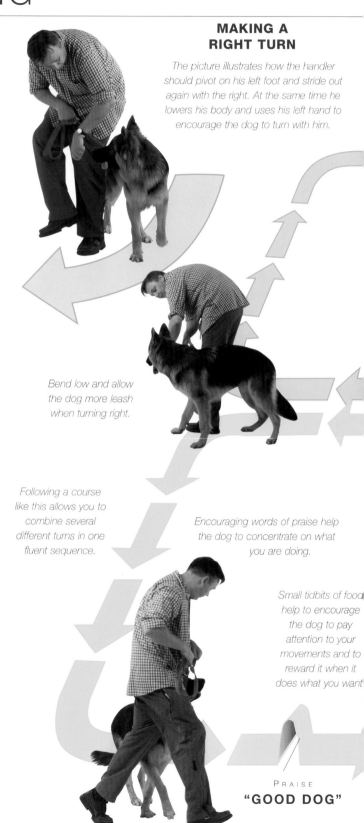

MAKING A RIGHT TURN

The picture illustrates how the handler should pivot on his left foot and stride out again with the right. At the same time he lowers his body and uses his left hand to encourage the dog to turn with him.

Bend low and allow the dog more leash when turning right.

Following a course like this allows you to combine several different turns in one fluent sequence.

Encouraging words of praise help the dog to concentrate on what you are doing.

Small tidbits of food help to encourage the dog to pay attention to your movements and to reward it when it does what you want

PRAISE
"GOOD DOG"

START

This square circuit allows you to practice a succession of turns.

MAKING A LEFT TURN

The left turn features a pivot on the left leg. In this case the right knee is raised and used as the body swivels to emphasize the change of direction.

The dog is doing well – it is nicely under control and paying attention to the handler.

Pat your knee to encourage obedience.

Walk off in a straight line commanding **"Heel."**

As the dog learns to stay close by your side, a bond of trust is built up between you.

The right knee makes it clear that you are turning left.

The right turn involves a left leg pivot. As you are turning away from the dog's line of motion, use hand signals and verbal encouragement to keep it attentive.

Note how the knee blocks the dog's contrary head movement.

Keeping an eye on your dog as you make straight transits helps it to become watchful of your movements.

HEELWORK IN THE STREET

Above: *Walking next to a fence is a good way of foiling a dog that wants to pull off to one side. A fence post is also the ideal spot on which to drop the leash when you need the dog to sit while you take a rest.*

Street Heelwork

Walking from your house to the park or through town is another important part of teaching a dog new rules of obedience. With dogs that tend to pull off to the left a good deal or dogs that don't concentrate at first, I will walk next to walls and fences quite closely to prevent any lateral straying. This means that the dog can now only pull forward or backward. If it pulls forward, I will about turn commanding **"Heel"** while offering a treat or squeaking the favored toy to gain the dog's attention. Many dogs soon catch on to changing direction quickly with you, lured by the reward and the vocal praise as they near your left side again.

For dogs that ignore these rewards — and many dogs do — snap the leash. When the dog feels the snap, it generally looks in your direction. At this point command **"Heel"** and tap your side while bending low. As the dog starts to align itself with you again, indulge in a little bit of amateur dramatics so the dog thinks that this is really fun. You must turn every time the dog surges. Repetition begins to teach the dog where you, the leader, want it to be in relation to you.

3
The squeak of the toy is the reward that lures the dog around as you change direction.

4
Praise the dog if it stays close by your left side.

74

Practice heel turns in three ten-minute lessons a day for up to seven days, or until your dog has learned to heel consistently. The sessions can be longer if they are part of a walk. Use a 1.2 m (4 ft.) leash.

When you come to curbs, crosswalks or need to stop, employ the Sit/Stay or Stand/Stay exercises to maintain control (see Chapter 9).

ENCOURAGING TURNS

START : 1
Another method of dealing with a dog that surges or pulls off to the left is to use a favorite toy as a lure to encourage it to stay close by your side.

2
A sharp squeak with the toy should be enough to regain the dog's attention. The handler here has the leash in her left hand as she feels more comfortable with the toy in her right.

COMMAND
"HEEL"

Some Heel Tips

• Change your daily route as often as possible. Dogs that cannot predict routine are less likely to pull.

• If your dog is particularly bad on any occasion, stop and tell the dog to **"Sit."** If necessary do this near a fencepost or railing over which you can drop the end loop of the leash. At least you can have a breather and collect your thoughts, and your dog will be very impressed with your firmness not to move. It doesn't make the connection that the leash is secured to the railing.

• Constantly executing right or left about turns when walking along sidewalks and adding frequent sit positions teaches the dog that a walk involves a set of rules that, when obeyed, bring rewards, not conflict. Dogs will generally prefer gentle praise, tidbits and the relaxed countenance you display when they behave well to prolonged stress and conflict.

• If your dog becomes bored while you are training in the yard or park, take out a favorite toy and throw the toy for the dog to retrieve. This often alleviates tension, and adds some fun at the end of a heel exercise. Dogs learn to associate the play time with the heel training.

TRAINING FOR CAR TRAVEL

1

The dog should be walking calmly to heel as you approach the car — no mad dashes!

2

Tell your dog to "Sit" at a little distance from the car. If the dog obeys, you may open the door.

Dog/Car Training

This section explains what to do if you have problems getting your dog to the car because it becomes over-excited. Before leaving the house have your car door closed, but not locked so that it is easy to open. Approach the car and then suddenly about turn and walk back to the house. Vary the door that you use and open the rear or side door. As the dog expects to leap in, command **"Heel"** and tap your left side. Walk away again and repeat this three or four times or until the dog calms down. Practice this many times over the course of a week or so, until order has been reestablished.

If possible, park your car next to a lamppost, picket fence or railing over which you can drop the leash and which allows your dog to get close to the door but not actually into the car. As the leash tightens as the dog strains against the post, command **"Sit."** Wait about a minute. Praise the dog if it sits quietly but ignore the dog if it gets excited. Only begin to take up the leash again if the dog is calm. After many repetitions and over many days your dog will start to realize that it

can't get into the car by pulling. Always remember to tell the dog to sit a short distance from the car. You may sometimes walk away from the car taking your dog with you to eliminate its sense of expectancy. Only after the dog has sat and you have said **"In"** does the dog get into the car.

At times you should even call your dog back out of the car several times so that it can never predict the routine. In time, the dog will become calm and learn this series of commands and actions: **"Sit"** — place leash on — **"Heel"** — walk to front door — you go through the door first — dog is called through with **"Heel"** — walk to car without pulling — **"Sit"** — dog sits on command next to car door — door is opened — dog is told **"In"** — dog gets in.

Right (1-4): You can deal with a dog that becomes overexcited as you approach a car by confusing its normal expectations. Just as it seems that you are about to open the car door, about turn, command "Heel" and walk away. Repeat this a few times – the dog should calm down as it will not know when the car door is really going to be opened.

3

*If the dog sits obediently as you open the door, command **"In."** Shut the door if the dog tries to enter before you say so.*

4

The dog gets in on your command – that's the new discipline. Every now and then call your dog out again and repeat the procedure. It helps if it cannot always predict your intentions.

2

"Heel"

4

TRAINING FOR CAR TRAVEL

1

*You must aim to keep equal control of the situation
when it is time to let your dog out of the car again.*

2

Open the car door and instruct the dog to **"Sit."**
You decide when the moment is right to let it out.

At the Park — Letting the Dog Out

For badly behaved dogs, especially large, strong ones,
place the dog's leash over a hook or handle inside the car
so that when you open the door, the dog cannot physically jump out. Tell the dog to **"Sit."** Wait with the door
open, then gently unhook the leash and when ready call
the dog out with **"Come."** As the dog gets out,
command **"Sit."** As the dog's front feet hit the ground
shorten the leash immediately so that you have more
control pulling the leash upward but not tightening it. Use
your Sit training techniques to complete the Sit. Now
position your dog by your left side with **"Heel"** and make
it sit again. When you are ready, head to the exercise
ground. Don't disconnect the dog's leash as soon as you
enter a field, park or recreational area. Walk at least 100 m
(300 ft.) into the park and then tell the dog to **"Sit."** Wait
a minute or so and then release the dog with **"Free."**
Most people with difficult dogs let them go immediately
because of their bad behavior, but this just teaches the
dog that it is released when it wants to be, rather than on
your command.

Walking with a Stroller

Once your dog is walking without pulling, you may
wish to walk the dog and your baby or young child
together. It's excellent for all concerned and builds up
a good relationship between child and dog.

The first rule is to walk with your dog on your left.
Initially, it helps to push an empty stroller along the
street for a few hundred yards while the dog gets used
to the noise and appearance of this unfamiliar object.
Command **"Heel"** in the normal way. Observe your
dog's reactions and encourage it with praise and a few
tidbits if it seems a little afraid of the stroller. Most
dogs quickly adapt. Only place your child in the stroller
and walk the dog together when the dog walks
perfectly alongside the stroller. **Never wrap the leash
around your hand or the stroller's handlebars** — if
the dog panics or takes fright, the consequences could
be awful. Push the stroller with your right hand and hold
the leash with your left on this occasion. Dogs quickly
adapt to watching the stroller being maneuvered and
alter their walking pace to suit your speed.

3

If the dog stays calm, pick up (or unhook) the leash and command **"Come."**

4

Make the dog **"Sit"** *as soon as it is out. Move off when you choose to.*

WALKING WITH A STROLLER

It is a good idea to habituate your dog to walking alongside an empty stroller before you repeat the exercise with a baby aboard. In this case, use one hand for the stroller or buggy, and one for the leash. Once the dog is fully trained, you can hold the leash in either hand. Encourage the dog with words of praise as it walks calmly beside you.

Heel Training — Review

• **"Heel"** means change of direction or stay by my side.

• Food tidbit and/or toy offered in front of the nose connects the command to a reward.

• Throwing the toy adds another reward and a fun game at the end of an exercise.

• You control getting in and out of the car by a set of linked actions.

This scene illustrates the importance of heelwork training — just imagine the mother's difficulties if the dog was pulling out of control.

PRAISE
"GOOD DOG"

FACE COLLARS

Face collars consist of an arrangement of straps that fit over a dog's muzzle linked to a collar that is secured around its neck. Take care how you introduce a dog to a face collar. They can cause stress initially, so you need to take things slowly.

Using Face Collars

So far our heel training exercises have concentrated on methods that you can teach your dog using a collar and leash. However, with very determined pullers you may need to use different equipment, such as a face collar or body harness. A face collar fits over the dog's muzzle, and it allows the dog's mouth to open as usual so that it can breathe normally. When the dog pulls ahead of its owner, the face collar tugs the dog's head back toward the owner, making it uncomfortable or awkward for the dog to pull. Face collars do work well on most, but not all, dogs, and I have found that determined or difficult dogs do settle down and learn not to pull. One drawback is that they can sometimes rub on the dog's face, causing some minor abrasion of the skin surface. However, fitted properly, they are without doubt an efficient way to stop a determined puller from stretching your arms.

It is very important to introduce the face collar to your dog slowly and to build good associations with the face collar in your dog's mind. Most people rush the introduction and then become upset at their dog's stressed reaction to it. Avoid this by doing the following.

First, get your dog to sit with a leash and collar on. Have several juicy tidbits on hand. Then place the face collar on your dog and reward it with a tidbit. Leave the face collar on your dog for a few minutes; give a food reward intermittently. Your dog should now associate having the face collar fitted with receiving a reward. This needs to be repeated three times a day for about ten minutes' duration over a period of three days. Next, attach the leash to the face collar and walk your dog a short distance around the house or yard; reward the dog at short intervals. If your dog panics or attempts to rub its head on the floor (which is normal), distract the dog with food and use your leash to make

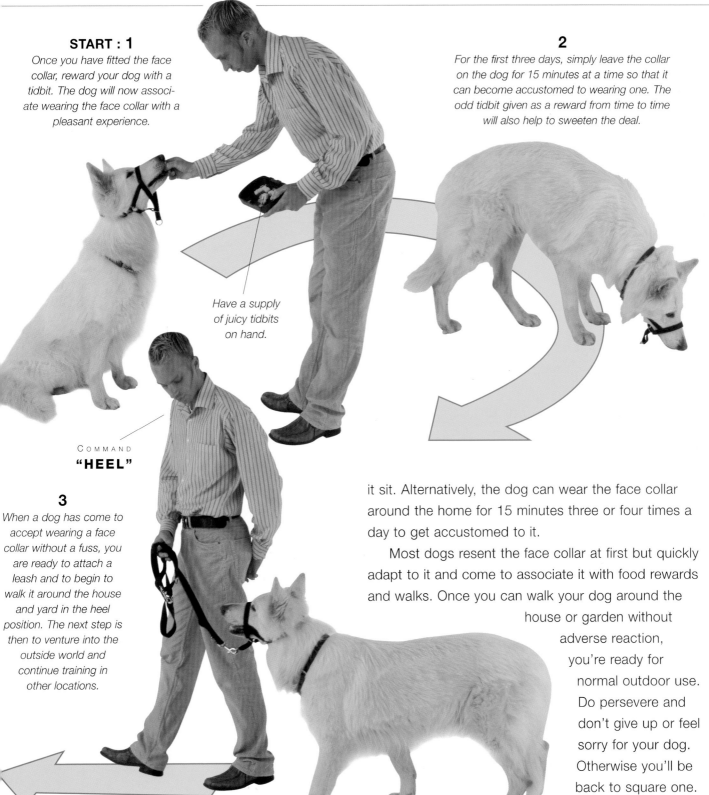

START : 1

Once you have fitted the face collar, reward your dog with a tidbit. The dog will now associate wearing the face collar with a pleasant experience.

Have a supply
of juicy tidbits
on hand.

2

For the first three days, simply leave the collar on the dog for 15 minutes at a time so that it can become accustomed to wearing one. The odd tidbit given as a reward from time to time will also help to sweeten the deal.

COMMAND
"HEEL"

3

When a dog has come to accept wearing a face collar without a fuss, you are ready to attach a leash and to begin to walk it around the house and yard in the heel position. The next step is then to venture into the outside world and continue training in other locations.

it sit. Alternatively, the dog can wear the face collar around the home for 15 minutes three or four times a day to get accustomed to it.

Most dogs resent the face collar at first but quickly adapt to it and come to associate it with food rewards and walks. Once you can walk your dog around the house or garden without adverse reaction, you're ready for normal outdoor use. Do persevere and don't give up or feel sorry for your dog. Otherwise you'll be back to square one.

OTHER TRAINING AIDS

Left: An anti-pulling harness typically uses thin straps that fit under the dog's front legs. If it chooses to pull strongly ahead while out walking, the straps exert pressure on the dog's armpits causing it some discomfort.

Right: Another make of harness reveals the basically similar way in which they both work.

Body Harnesses

There are also harnesses available to help stop dogs pulling. They are not to be confused with a general dog harness, which helps dogs to pull more effectively. A typical anti-pulling harness has thin cords that pass under the dog's front legs so that when the dog surges ahead, the cords pull tight on the dog's armpits, causing physical discomfort. When the dog stops pulling, the discomfort disappears. The dog dictates its own comfort level and many dogs quickly stop pulling this way.

The High Check Collar

This training technique should only be applied to dogs that are very difficult to train to heel and that have failed to respond to the other methods you may have tried. It is only appropriate with medium to large dogs, but it is a very effective way of stopping these types of dogs pulling. The high check gets its name because a slip collar is placed high on the dog's neck just below the ears. This slip collar is made of thick round nylon and is designed to tighten on the dog's neck if it pulls. It is kept high in this position throughout the walk because it prevents the dog from using its neck fully as a pulling lever. It also stops the dog lowering its head

This is how the harness being fitted (right) appears "out of the box."

into a low driving position in order to use its body power and neck muscles to pull you forward and force its way ahead.

You operate the high check more or less like a normal leash and fixed collar, but instead of having a loose leash between the collar ring and the leash clip, the distance between your hand holding the leash and the high check collar attached to the dog is only about 30 cm (12 in.). In other words the leash is kept very short, but not excessively taut (it has a little slack in it). If the leash is left too loose, the high check collar will slip lower down on the dog's neck into the normal position of a collar and become ineffective.

When the dog attempts to surge ahead, it is simply not able to use its body power, and at the same time the collar becomes uncomfortable on its neck when it pulls. This functions in the same way as a face collar, which pulls the dog's face to the side, or a body harness, which tightens on the dog's armpits when it pulls. The dog discovers that life is uncomfortable if it

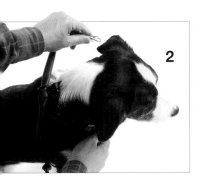

Above (1-5): An anti-pulling harness is usually fitted in the manner illustrated here. Firstly the collar is clipped around the dog's neck (1) and then the two underleg straps are passed through the appropriate buckles (2), under the dog's front legs (3) and fastened to clips on the underside of the collar (4). Finally a tensioner slide can be moved to adjust the overall tightness of the harness (5). Don't make it too tight — it should only be uncomfortable when the dog pulls.

Below and right: A high check collar is positioned further up the dog's neck than usual. It inhibits its ability to lower its head and drive forward and so helps prevent pulling.

Only allow about 30 cm (12 in.) of leash between your hand and a high check collar. But don't haul the leash tight — there needs to be a little slack so the collar is loose.

Slip collar position

Normal collar position

pulls, but that it's comfortable when it doesn't. The dog will soon learn the difference and, if simultaneously provided with a nice reward for not pulling, will soon be walking obediently at your side.

Once a dog has learned not to pull on a walk, you can allow the slip collar to fall back into a normal collar position or even preferably switch back to a conventional fixed collar.

One word of warning: Never use the high check on puppies or toy breeds. It is not suitable for small dogs.

CHAPTER NINE

The Stay Positions

The Sit, Stand, Down and Stay Positions

Teaching dogs to sit, stand and lie down on command are excellent exercises that will be useful throughout the dog's life. Untrained dogs, like badly behaved children, are not welcome in many places. A trained dog knows what is and what is not allowed and tends to be more relaxed, content and most of all controllable in our complex and demanding society. So you can begin training these three exercises in the knowledge that your dog's education is developing fast.

Initially the Sit, Stand and Down positions will be taught so that the dog understands clearly which position relates to which command. Then, we will complete the lessons with the Stay exercise in all three positions, which broadens the dog's overall obedience plan.

All this training begins on Day 1 and lasts for three 15-minute lessons daily. Initially these can be organized around the home and yard, while the third lesson of the day can take place just before or during a walk. Some owners who have dogs that are unmanageable outside the home may wish to do all of their training in the home for the first week until they have instilled some semblance of obedience — this is fine as long as the dog gets plenty of exercise through games after each training session.

If your dog has very ingrained bad habits — maybe it is a rescue dog or has not had adequate formal training — the problems may be embedded. A good example is a dog that has not responded to the recall command for many years, meaning that the handler has to chase and catch the dog. The animal may only have been exercised in places where it met few dogs,

or you may have deliberately avoided other dogs to prevent the problem occurring. This is really masking the problem, but it is often how many owners deal with an untrained dog. Or you may own a dog that pulls on the leash for a long time while being walked. The learned behavior will be embedded and the pulling will be a part of the dog's natural routine that it has practiced many hundreds of times. In a perverse way this is also dog training — albeit training of the wrong kind. The 21-Day Training Program should be able to correct this.

With all the following exercises, it is important to command then reward, and to allow quiet pauses in between so that the exercise is not a continuous ramble of words, which only makes learning more difficult for the dog.

The Sit Position (puppy safe)

Teaching your dog to sit is without a doubt one of the easiest lessons to accomplish, and most people have little trouble with it. Dogs are lower to the ground than us and they tend to look upward at our faces. This articulation of their body helps us to encourage the Sit. A leash and collar can be used but most dogs learn the Sit just as well without one.

Puppies learn to sit quickly and a choice tidbit or the sight of its food bowl across the kitchen creates great excitement as you assume the role of surrogate mother. As you hold the food bowl or tidbit just above the pup's face, two things should happen beside some vocalization of excitement: The pup will naturally sit and you should simultaneously deliver the crisp command **"Sit"** and then offer the reward you have in

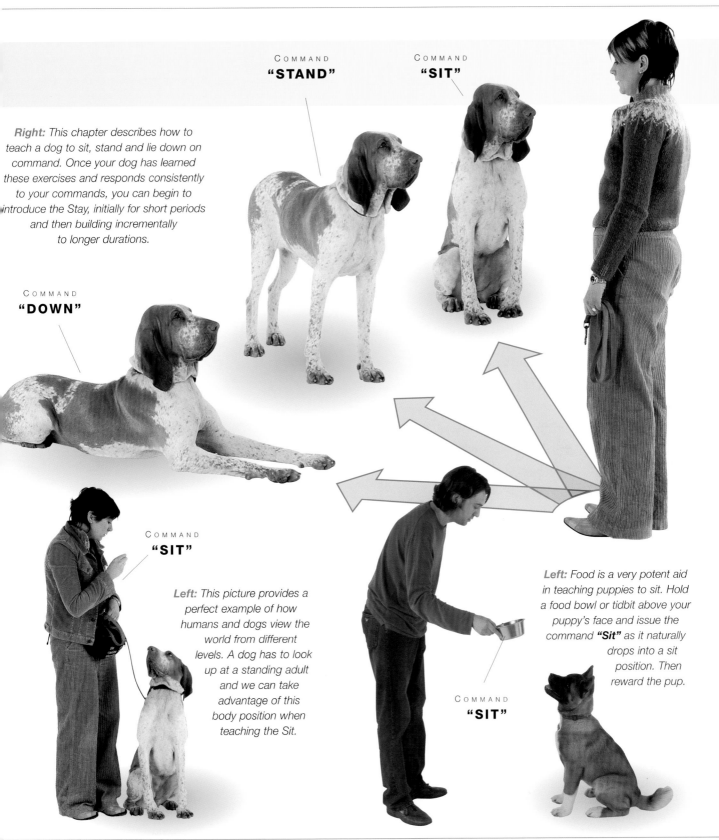

C O M M A N D
"STAND"

C O M M A N D
"SIT"

Right: This chapter describes how to teach a dog to sit, stand and lie down on command. Once your dog has learned these exercises and responds consistently to your commands, you can begin to introduce the Stay, initially for short periods and then building incrementally to longer durations.

C O M M A N D
"DOWN"

C O M M A N D
"SIT"

Left: This picture provides a perfect example of how humans and dogs view the world from different levels. A dog has to look up at a standing adult and we can take advantage of this body position when teaching the Sit.

C O M M A N D
"SIT"

Left: Food is a very potent aid in teaching puppies to sit. Hold a food bowl or tidbit above your puppy's face and issue the command **"Sit"** as it naturally drops into a sit position. Then reward the pup.

TEACHING THE SIT

your hand. Days later, the pup should be sitting even before the command is given thanks to repetition, reward and its observance of your body language.

So why don't dogs sit when told to and why do so many people have difficulty getting a reliable Sit out of a puppy or adult dog? They certainly know what "Sit" means.

Let's examine the situation where you taught the puppy. You were in a quiet training location, e.g., the kitchen. You used a powerful reward, and a clear command was followed by praise and the reward of the food. When the dog is in other rooms, the yard or a park, the greatest challenge to you as the trainer is to obtain the same results considering the amazing array of distractions that will vie for the dog's attention. Other dogs, people's scents and actions all distract the dog. Like children, dogs live in the present and it is a good idea to keep this thought in mind throughout your training — the dog and the child inhabit a simple, uncomplicated world. These distractions apply to all the training programs, but examining them from the dog's perspective, I will explain several methods that will enable you to teach your dog to sit, stand and lie down on command.

The Sit Using Food (puppy safe)

Food is a powerful means to attract a dog's attention and is the first arrow in my quiver as a trainer. Start in a quiet room and hold the tidbit just above your dog's nose. When it walks forward eagerly to get the treat, command **"Sit"** and slightly pass the hand holding the treat up and over the dog's head so that it actually needs to look upward to keep its eye on the treat. Most dogs will naturally fall into the sit position. As they do so, immediately give the treat. So you have the command **"Sit"** and then a treat delivered virtually within a second or two.

SIT USING FOOD

START : 1

We exploit the technique illustrated on the previous page with the puppy and food bowl to teach the Sit to an adult dog, but this time using a tidbit. Attract the dog's attention and get it to come to you by offering a food treat.

COMMAND
"COME"

**SIT USING FOOD
(for smaller dogs)**

COMMAND
"COME"

2

As the dog approaches, bend down and offer the treat just in front of and above the dog's nose.

COMMAND
"SIT"

3

*Then command **"Sit"** and pass your hand up above the dog's head. As it looks up to follow the treat, it should drop into a sit position.*

START : 1

When training puppies or smaller dogs like this dachshund, it helps at first to work in a kneeling or crouching position as the dog is going to be fairly close to the floor even when standing.

COMMAND
"SIT"

2

By moving your hand up over the dog's head, it can be encouraged to drop into a sit position while its gaze rests on the tidbit. Give the dog the food reward and a few words of praise as soon as it has sat obediently.

TEACHING THE SIT

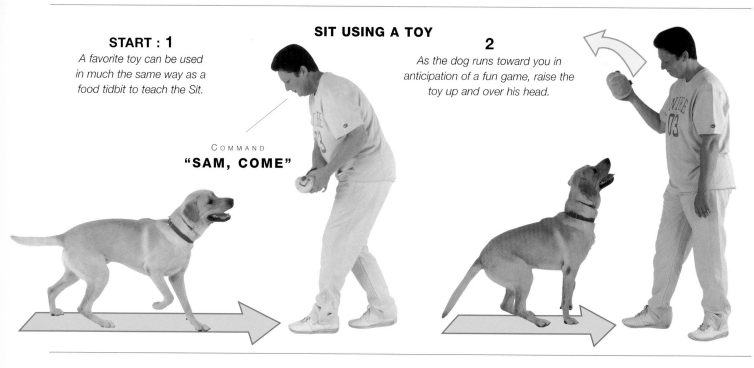

START : 1

A favorite toy can be used in much the same way as a food tidbit to teach the Sit.

SIT USING A TOY

COMMAND
"SAM, COME"

2

As the dog runs toward you in anticipation of a fun game, raise the toy up and over his head.

If working with smaller breeds or puppies, you may need to be in a crouching position to help lead the dog's body into the natural position with the food treat. Repeat the exercise several times during each of your three lessons a day and at feeding times. Using your feeding routine will help reinforce the Sit training.

The Sit Using Toys

If your dog is toy-oriented, then select the dog's favorite toy and use the toy like a food tidbit. Position yourself in the same way holding the toy aloft and when the dog sits immediately throw the toy. The chase is the reward for the dog entering the sit position on command. It does no harm at this stage to have a thin, light leash attached to the dog so that you are able to recover the toy from an eager dog wishing to play chase with its new trophy. If you have already taught the Recall (see Chapter 10), then the leash is not needed. Remember, as with all toy training, keep the toys locked away from the dog at all other times during the entire training course. It helps keep the dog keen.

The Ignore and Sit (puppy safe)

This approach truly shows dog training psychology in action. It does require patience on your behalf, but when applied consistently it trains a dog to sit in a more natural and less direct manner. When you first enter a room where your dog is and it comes over to say "hello" just command **"Sit"** and look directly at the dog holding your empty hand upward though with no treat. The dog is now learning signals and commands simultaneously.

If the dog sits, give it a stroke and a little praise. If it immediately moves, ignore it again and carry on with your routine. "In your face," dominant or spoiled dogs used to having lavish attention tend to need a lot of interaction. After about ten minutes when you can see the dog out of the corner of your eye, call it to you with a **"Come"** command. As it arrives, command **"Sit"** again. If it becomes too excited or just stares at you with that big doggy grin, walk off again and ignore it. The dog will not expect this and they will quickly catch on that you now decide when attention is given, and praise will come when they sit on command.

3

Command **"Sit"** as the dog's haunches settle on the ground. Praise him.

COMMAND
"SIT"

COMMAND
"FETCH"

4

Then quickly throw the toy for the dog to chase. Play is the reward for sitting when commanded.

START : 1

In this exercise you introduce a hand signal in conjunction with the **"Sit"** command. Tell your dog to **"Sit"** as he runs up to greet you.

COMMAND
"SIT"

IGNORE AND SIT

A dog should only move from a sit, stand or down position when you give the command **"Free,"** or if you use another command like **"Fetch."** The dog should never be allowed to move of its own volition. Do remember to release the dog with **"Free."**

COMMAND
"SIT"

4

The dog learns that praise only comes when he assumes the sit position on command.

2

If the dog just plays around and pays no attention to the command, studiously ignore him and carry on with your normal day-to-day business.

3

A few minutes later, call the dog to you and command **"Sit"** again. If this doesn't work, ignore him again and repeat the exercise until you do achieve success.

TEACHING THE SIT

The Sit Using a Hook

For very boisterous or very large breeds of dog that jump up a good deal and are hard to control because of their exuberant behavior, some short-term extra equipment is needed. These dogs are often rescue dogs or dogs that have just not learned that you don't like their aberrant behavior, however well intentioned it is.

Fix hooks securely in several locations around the house — into baseboards or screwed to walls. In the yard you can use firm supports like fence posts or a secure wall. These are useful when trying to teach an excited dog the Sit. Take the dog's leash — this generally arouses great interest — and attach the leash to the dog.

Make sure you are next to a hook fixture. Hold the food or toy and command **"Sit"** — simultaneously drop the leash over the hook so that you have your hands free (except for the treat). As the dog feels constrained, you can step back and then forward again completely in charge of the situation. When the dog assumes the Sit, give it the treat. This method prevents the dog climbing all over you, and reduces the need for you to manhandle the dog (which in most cases is the reaction the dog has learned to obtain — the reward of body touch and a rough, fun game).

Through repetition around the yard and the house, the dog soon learns that by sitting calmly it receives a treat. Using different locations teaches the dog that this command can take place anywhere around the home.

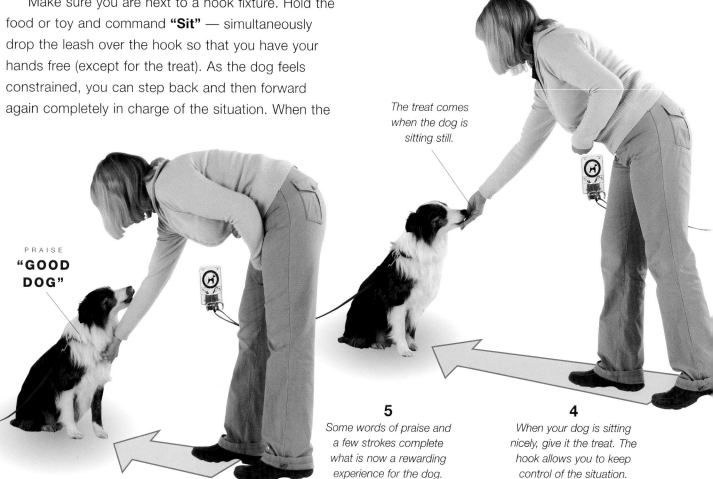

The treat comes when the dog is sitting still.

PRAISE
"GOOD DOG"

5
Some words of praise and a few strokes complete what is now a rewarding experience for the dog.

4
When your dog is sitting nicely, give it the treat. The hook allows you to keep control of the situation.

Below: When training very lively dogs, which are liable to jump all over you and generally create chaos, a hook that restrains the dog and allows you to control its movements can be a valuable training tool.

START : 1
Begin by dropping the end of the leash over a conveniently situated hook.

Use a food treat to focus the dog's attention on you.

C O M M A N D
"SIT"

2
*You now have your hands free and can stand just out of the dog's range in quiet control of the situation. Command **"Sit."***

3
By rocking forward and coaxing the dog with the tidbit, you will be able to encourage it to fall into a sit.

6
Praise a dog that does well and then take a bit of time out. Training until a dog becomes bored and inattentive is counterproductive.

TEACHING THE SIT

START : 1
This sit takes advantage of the fact that dogs are lower to the ground than us and tend to look upward at our faces. This body articulation encourages the sit position. Call your dog and at the same time run a few paces backward.

COMMAND
"COME"

2
As the dog nears you, take a pace forward and incline your upper body to lean over it.

START : 1
Practicing the Sit exercise presupposes that your dog will "play along" and remain attentive to you. Of course, some dogs are not like this — they have their minds on other things, are hard to control and tend to run off. This is where the use of a leash allows you to keep control.

The Sit: Forward and Backward (puppy safe)

This style of training is again quite subtle and relates to your deportment and body language. It works on all types of dogs but is especially good for dogs that are sensitive or deferential and dogs that tend to get panicky if you overhandle them. It can be used in conjunction with some of the other methods described.

Simply call your dog to you in a room and, as the dog approaches you, run a few steps backward. This should encourage your dog to run forward to you — as it does so take a step toward the dog and slightly lean over it. The sudden change of direction by the leader causes the dog to adopt a deferential position as it has to look vertically up into your face. If the command **"Sit"** is given during this action, the dog

3
*While leaning forward give the command **"Sit"** and at the same time use the hand signal for the Sit to reinforce the verbal command. The dog should fall back into a sit position.*

COMMAND
"SIT"

4
Finish the exercise with words of praise and plenty of pats and strokes.

will normally sit. If that happens, praise it lavishly and walk off. Repeat several more times.

The Sit: Leash and Collar Style (puppy safe)

Using the leash and collar is again useful with dogs that tend to run off or are difficult to control. Hold the leash in your right hand and have some food treats available in a belt bag or a suitable pocket. Repeat the advice given in the Sit Using Food section, but now add the leash control.

Once your dog has the general idea of the Sit — which on average takes about 30 sit practices over a few days — and you are confident enough to progress, you can begin to teach the Sit/Stay. You are now adding a link to the Sit and we will do the same later on for the next two positions: the Stand and the Down.

COMMAND
"SIT"

2

*Call your dog for a treat and as it approaches command **"Sit"** and move your hand over the dog's head.*

3

The dog will look up and naturally drop into a sit position. If it does this, give it the treat immediately. The sit and the reward are linked in its mind.

PRAISE
"GOOD DOG"

4

You're happy — the dog has behaved; the dog is happy — it's getting stroked.

INTRODUCING THE SIT/STAY

START : 1

*Once your dog takes up and remains in the sit position consistently, you are ready to introduce the **"Stay"** command.*

The flat of the hand signals that the dog should stay.

COMMAND
"STAY"

SIT/STAY WITH HAND SIGNALS
2

To begin with, only move about a pace or so away from your dog. You are really trying to reinforce the time that the dog will remain in the Sit while you remove yourself from its immediate presence. You will practice the exercise at longer distances later in the 21-day program.

COMMAND
"STAY"

Sit/Stay — Introducing Hand Signals

Tell your dog to sit and, placing the flat of your hand in front of the dog as an additional signal, command **"Stay."** Move no more than one step away from the dog's side. Wait about three seconds and say **"Stay"** once more, then move back to the dog's side. Praise the dog immediately using voice and touch. It is not necessary to offer food every time, but perhaps every third or fourth time as you practice the lesson. Always allow some slack in the leash so that it never tugs on

the dog's neck, as most dogs will move toward you if this occurs, however mild the tug. If the dog becomes too excited when you praise it or offer a treat, only use verbal praise and at a level that will not excite the dog and encourage it to move.

The important part of the training exercises relating to the Stay position is the time that the dog is left in that position, not the distance that you move away from the dog. Strange as it may seem, most people seem to want to walk a fair distance from the dog

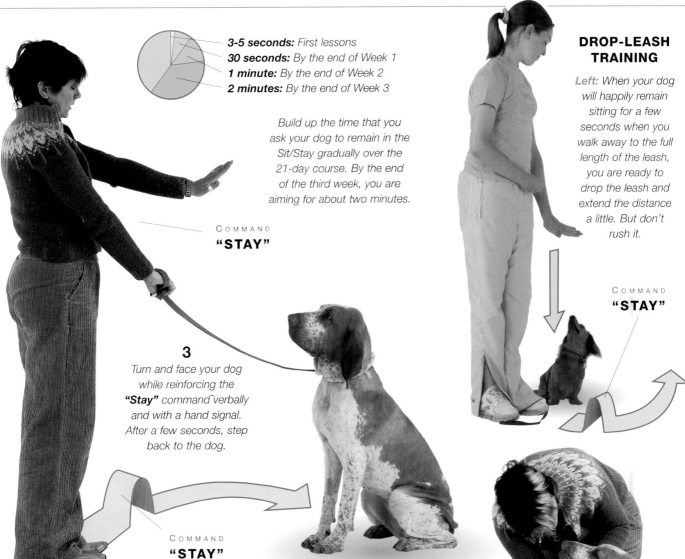

3-5 seconds: First lessons
30 seconds: By the end of Week 1
1 minute: By the end of Week 2
2 minutes: By the end of Week 3

Build up the time that you ask your dog to remain in the Sit/Stay gradually over the 21-day course. By the end of the third week, you are aiming for about two minutes.

COMMAND
"STAY"

DROP-LEASH TRAINING

Left: When your dog will happily remain sitting for a few seconds when you walk away to the full length of the leash, you are ready to drop the leash and extend the distance a little. But don't rush it.

COMMAND
"STAY"

3

*Turn and face your dog while reinforcing the **"Stay"** command verbally and with a hand signal. After a few seconds, step back to the dog.*

COMMAND
"STAY"

4

If it has gone well, give the dog lots of praise and affection. This is the first step on a journey that you will take together, so it pays to make it fun.

rather than wait for a period nearby. Time and solidity is what is required as a first stage in this Sit/Stay, and if you can reach the end of your leash by the third training lesson on Day 1, you're doing well.

You should not attempt to drop the leash until your dog comfortably accepts you walking away from it to the limit of the leash and then walking back after a few seconds without it moving. And it must wait for your praise or the occasional tidbit.

EXTENDING THE SIT/STAY

START : 1

Once your dog is pretty solid in the basic Sit/Stay, you can think about extending the distance to which you walk and returning in a circular path.

COMMAND
"STAY"

2

*Start with the dog sitting on your left-hand side. Give a firm **"Stay"** command, use the hand signal to reinforce the order, and step off from the start position. In this example the handler is using a 3 m (10 ft.) leash.*

COMMAND
"STAY"

COMMAND
"STAY"

Stay and Circle on the Leash

Many dogs that remain steady at a distance of a few feet seem to lose the Stay when you decide to walk back to the dog in a counterclockwise circle. Their little heads spin trying to keep you in sight and suddenly their rump moves from the sitting position. The best way to remedy this is to command **"Stay"** sharply just as you are about to walk around your dog counter-clockwise — continue to walk around the dog and return to the dog on its right-hand side. When the exercise is complete, you and the dog should be facing the same way with it on your left still sitting obediently.

When returning to a dog that is in the stay position — be it the Sit, Stand or Down — many people hesitate if the dog begins to move or looks as if it will

do so. They thereby take much longer to return, which makes the Stay a longer exercise in duration than it should be. This is unhelpful in these early learning stages. Always move quickly, not hesitatingly.

So now let's review the sit/stay actions in order. Stand beside your dog as if about to heel off. Tell the dog to sit and stay. Walk to the end of the leash, letting it out as you do so and, if the dog does not move, face the dog for a second or two, then immediately return using the same route. Give the dog one more command just as you return to emphasize that you want it to **"Stay."** Then quickly bend down and praise the dog. The lesson is complete. For variety repeat it in different locations in the house and yard.

TAY AND CIRCLE ON A LEASH

3

Walk out to the full length of the leash and then turn and face the dog who ought to be still sitting patiently in the sit position that it started in.

Stay exercises require a dog to curb its natural instincts and remain focused on a specific command. So let the dog enjoy your praise at the end – he deserves to let off a little steam.

C O M M A N D
"STAY"

4

*Command **"Stay"** again, and after waiting for a few seconds begin to walk back to the dog.*

5

*Give another **"Stay"** command as you start to walk around the back of the dog.*

6

The point when you pass behind the dog and out of its view is critical. Don't dawdle at this stage or the dog's concentration may start to waver.

7

You should end up where you started with the dog sitting quietly on your left. When you manage this, you can both feel pleased with yourselves.

C O M M A N D
"STAY"

EXTENDING THE SIT/STAY

Sit/Stay — Time and Distance Training

Once your dog is staying reliably at a distance of 1 m (3 ft.) or so, increase the time span of the exercise to about two minutes, but still at the same short distance — this is critical to future training stability. You can do this by increments of about 30 seconds per day. Do not try to increase the time too quickly, as this may ruin the continuing positive train-ing and the rewards that the dog associates with staying in the sit position. Dogs learn quicker if they are rewarded continually for doing it right, rather than if their training is inter-mittently interrupted for correction because their owners are trying to run before they can walk.

Once your dog is staying each and every time for at least a minute, you're making good progress. Often in training you will find that a dog that has been reliable at two minutes will suddenly begin to move for no apparent reason. Don't despair. Just practice a few lessons at 30 seconds and when the dog is proficient again at 30 seconds or so, begin to increase the time back up to two minutes again. That's just they way dogs learn at times. It's not a major problem.

I only begin increasing distance once the dog will stay consistently at about 2 m (6 ft.) and for two minutes. I begin to increase the

COMMAND
"STAY"

START : 1

As you start to increase the time of a sit/stay, just stand a few feet away from your dog. Extra distance will be added when the dog stays reliably for two minutes.

Gradually increase the duration of the Sit/Stays to around two minutes over the three weeks.

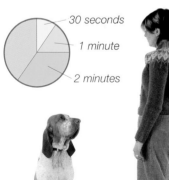

- 30 seconds
- 1 minute
- 2 minutes

distance by about a couple of meters per day until I have reached a distance of 10 m (30 ft.) or so. Again, as with the time duration, if a dog that has been reasonably reliable at say 5 m (15 ft.), suddenly begins to follow you or move from the sit/stay position, simply revert to a more manageable distance — say 2 m (6 ft.) — until you and the dog are back on track. Remember, a dog that stays consis-tently at a short distance and for a short time reliably will end up a well-trained dog. A good trainer knows when to make training easier for the dog to rebuild its confidence, as opposed to being insistent. Later in the chapter, there is more information on time and distance training in the various stay positions outside of the home.

2

When you return at the end of the Stay, walk in a counterclockwise direction around the dog in the way illustrated in the exercise on the previous page.

COMMAND
"STAY"

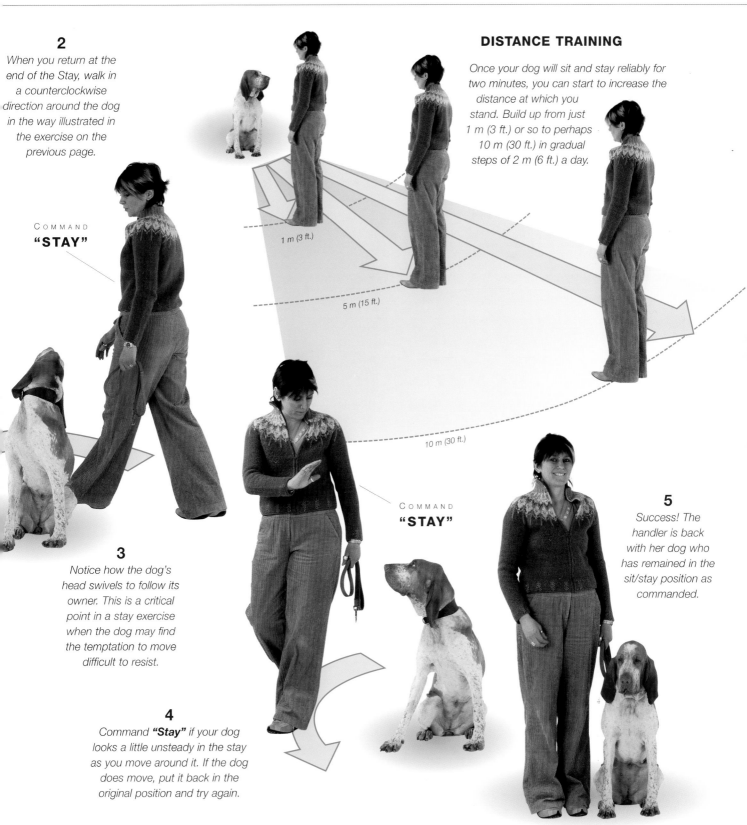

1 m (3 ft.)

5 m (15 ft.)

10 m (30 ft.)

DISTANCE TRAINING

Once your dog will sit and stay reliably for two minutes, you can start to increase the distance at which you stand. Build up from just 1 m (3 ft.) or so to perhaps 10 m (30 ft.) in gradual steps of 2 m (6 ft.) a day.

COMMAND
"STAY"

3

Notice how the dog's head swivels to follow its owner. This is a critical point in a stay exercise when the dog may find the temptation to move difficult to resist.

4

*Command **"Stay"** if your dog looks a little unsteady in the stay as you move around it. If the dog does move, put it back in the original position and try again.*

5

Success! The handler is back with her dog who has remained in the sit/stay position as commanded.

TEACHING THE STAND

The Stand Position

This position is most useful for dogs; it helps with grooming, veterinary inspection and when stopping at a cross-walk. It is useful to command the dog to stand at the curb, especially on mucky, rainy days when the sit position would get the dog's rump dirty.

The stand position is also useful when going through doors or if you need to stop and go while negotiating pedestrian traffic or similar obstacles. Show dogs are always taught to stand, as this is the glamor position exhibitors use for dog shows. The stand is also a position where your command should be crisp but not too loud. Any indication of verbal correction will often send a dog into a sit or a down to escape what they assume will be their leader's overt stern-ness — even when none is coming. So take stand

START : 1

You do not need a leash for this basic stand exercise, and it's simple to practice it around the house or yard whenever you like. Equip yourself with some choice tidbits and then call your dog to come to you.

The dog approaches when its owner calls.

C O M M A N D
"COME"

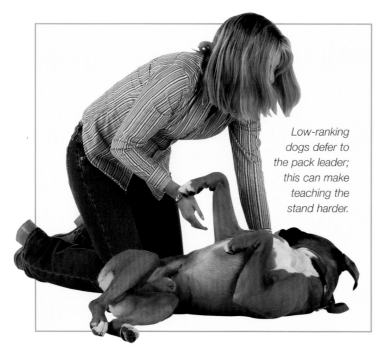

Low-ranking dogs defer to the pack leader; this can make teaching the stand harder.

training more gently. Also don't let your dog linger in the stand position for more than a few seconds in the first training lessons.

The Stand Using Turn and Food (puppy safe)

As most dogs are taught the Sit first, the Stand can be a little confusing for them. But including this exercise in your daily schedule is fine. Most dogs learn the Stand quite quickly, but less confident or low-ranking dogs often prefer to sit or lie down in case you — the pack leader — admonish them for standing too tall for their pack position. If this is the case with your dog, then be succinct but gentle. Definitely do not use force or the dog will immediately try to get even lower to avoid your displeasure.

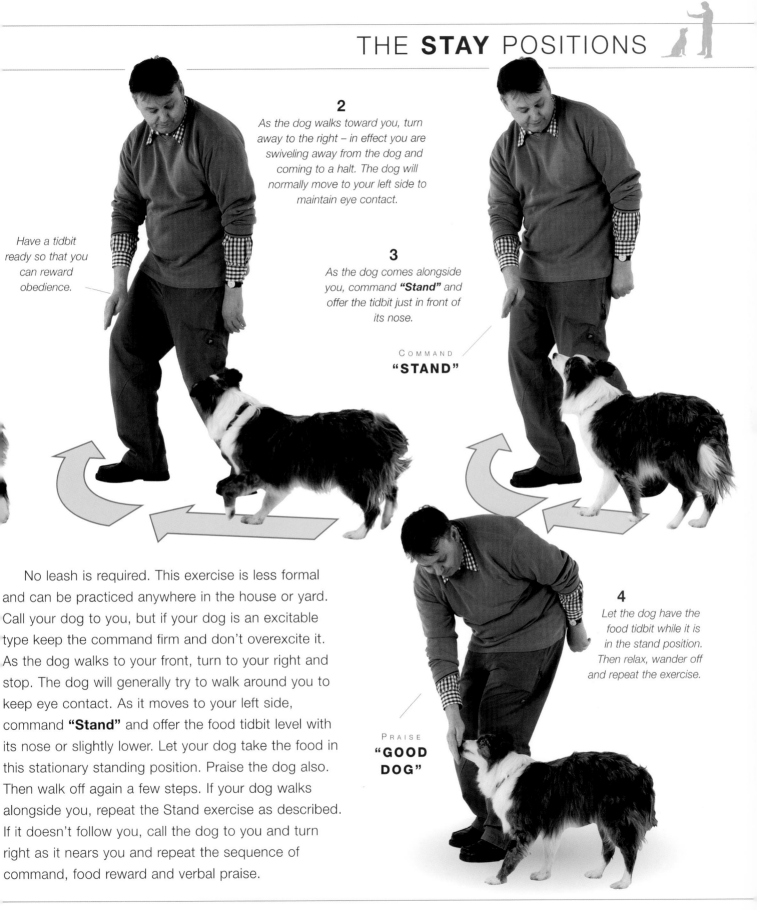

2

As the dog walks toward you, turn away to the right – in effect you are swiveling away from the dog and coming to a halt. The dog will normally move to your left side to maintain eye contact.

Have a tidbit ready so that you can reward obedience.

3

*As the dog comes alongside you, command **"Stand"** and offer the tidbit just in front of its nose.*

COMMAND
"STAND"

4

Let the dog have the food tidbit while it is in the stand position. Then relax, wander off and repeat the exercise.

PRAISE
"GOOD DOG"

No leash is required. This exercise is less formal and can be practiced anywhere in the house or yard. Call your dog to you, but if your dog is an excitable type keep the command firm and don't overexcite it. As the dog walks to your front, turn to your right and stop. The dog will generally try to walk around you to keep eye contact. As it moves to your left side, command **"Stand"** and offer the food tidbit level with its nose or slightly lower. Let your dog take the food in this stationary standing position. Praise the dog also. Then walk off again a few steps. If your dog walks alongside you, repeat the Stand exercise as described. If it doesn't follow you, call the dog to you and turn right as it nears you and repeat the sequence of command, food reward and verbal praise.

TEACHING THE STAND

The Stand Using Collar and Leash

The training method just described can be repeated using a collar and leash. You can simply walk around the house in the heel position and then stop, simultaneously commanding **"Stand"** and immediately offering the treat as before. It is critical not to delay the reward with the Stand otherwise many dogs will automatically sit, as that is how they have received treats in the other training lessons. New commands are just new sounds to them and have no meaning until the link with a physical position is established.

The Stand Using Toys (puppy safe)

It's optional whether you use a collar and leash for this exercise — it really depends on how calm or excitable your dog is. A toy can be useful for teaching the stand position. The appearance of the toy excites the dog.

Once you have shown the toy just out of reach of the dog's jaws tell it to **"Stand."** Wait a few seconds and then throw the toy as a reward. Once you have the toy back, repeat the lesson. You should also lengthen the duration of the Stand lesson over many repetitions. Within a week you should have your dog standing for a maximum of ten seconds at this early stage before throwing the toy again.

The Stand, Touch and Tickle (puppy safe)

This is my favorite method and without a doubt a very successful way of teaching the Stand. I use the collar and leash to walk the dog in the heel position around the yard or house. I halt and gently command **"Stand"** and simultaneously I place my left hand just under the dog's belly. This is a definite touch, but not a grab. Most dogs seem to freeze when you do this much as they do when dogs sniff each other's underside. I am taking advantage of this natural reaction to touch this area. As soon as the dog freezes or just before it turns to see what you are up to, I quickly move my left hand to tickle the dog's back just above its tail for one second.

So I command **"Stand,"** take one extra step forward after the command to allow the dog time to stop, touch its underside, tickle its back and praise all within a few seconds. Speed is essential. I then briskly command **"Heel"** and walk off again only to repeat the exercise several more times. Because different dogs are sensitive in different ways, you may need to adjust the touch and tickle method accordingly. Don't let the dog become overexcited. This training method certainly helps prevent dogs sitting all the time,

START : 1

The method of teaching the Stand with a turn and food reward illustrated on the previous page can also be used with a collar and leash.

STAND USING COLLAR AND LEAD

COMMAND

"STAND"

2

*While walking, stop, command **"Stand"** and offer the treat just in front of the dog's nose. Then move off and repeat.*

START : 1

You can also use a favorite toy to teach a dog to adopt a stand position.

COMMAND
"STAND"

STAND USING A TOY

2 and **3**

Let the dog chase and retrieve the toy as a reward for obeying the stand training. Then repeat the lesson.

Use your left hand to tickle the dog on his back just above his tail.

STAND, TOUCH AND TICKLE

START : 1

To train using the stand, touch and tickle method, begin by walking your dog to heel in the normal way. Then halt and command the dog to *"Stand."*

COMMAND
"HEEL"

COMMAND
"STAND"

3

Now swiftly move your hand and tickle the dog's back toward the top of its tail. This acts as a way of stabilizing the dog in the stand position. Praise the dog for its obedience, command **"Heel"** and walk off. After a short while, repeat the exercise.

2

When the dog comes to a halt, quickly touch its underside. This usually causes the dog to freeze in the stationary position.

STANDS AND STAND/STAYS

which is often a problem encountered by people trying to teach the Stand.

The Stand Using a Hook

We can use a leash, collar and hook fixed to a wall to teach the Stand. This approach is especially useful for dogs that get overexcited or take time to calm down when food is produced. Labradors come to mind here.

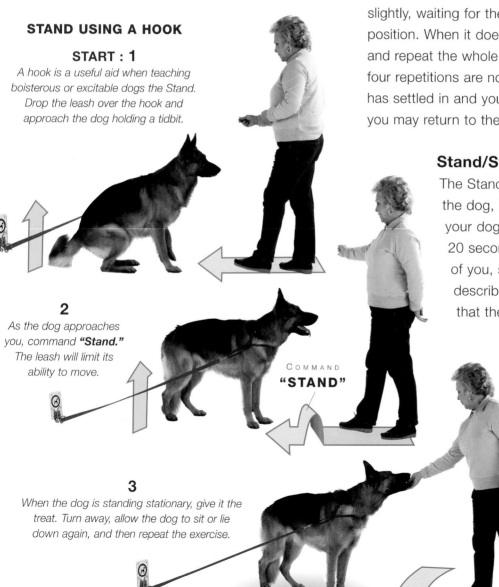

STAND USING A HOOK

START : 1

A hook is a useful aid when teaching boisterous or excitable dogs the Stand. Drop the leash over the hook and approach the dog holding a tidbit.

2

*As the dog approaches you, command **"Stand."** The leash will limit its ability to move.*

COMMAND
"STAND"

3

When the dog is standing stationary, give it the treat. Turn away, allow the dog to sit or lie down again, and then repeat the exercise.

With smaller breeds you will need to adopt a lower posture in the early stages of training so you don't dominate or tower over them.

Place your dog on the leash and attach it to the hook. Approach the dog with the food tidbit and, as the dog walks a step or two toward you, command **"Stand"** as it comes to a halt at the end of the now taut leash. Give a tidbit and turn and walk away slightly, waiting for the dog to relax into the down or sit position. When it does, walk back to the dog again and repeat the whole procedure once more. Three or four repetitions are normally enough. Once the idea has settled in and your dog seems to understand you, you may return to the other stand training styles.

Stand/Stay

The Stand/Stay, where you actually leave the dog, has some use on occasion. Once your dog stands consistently for at least 20 seconds next to your side or in front of you, simply follow the same format as described in the Sit/Stay routines except that the dog is in the stand position.

Don't make the dog stand for more than 30 seconds if you walk off, as it's not comfortable over a long period of time. There is no need to train a dog to stand for more than one minute.

The Stand Position — Problem Solving

My dog keeps sitting

You may be overpowering the dog. Don't tower over sensitive, low-ranking dogs as it makes them assume a lower position, slowing down the training. Dogs naturally learn the Sit quicker than the Stand, so when teaching the Stand, practice three stands for every sit initially until the stand is more stable.

My dog lies down

Use a leash and collar. Every time the dog attempts to lie down, tap your side and say **"Heel"** excitedly and move off swiftly for about 2 m (6 ft.). As the dog nears your side, repeat the **"Stand"** command. Never drag the dog upward with the leash, as it ruins the stand training.

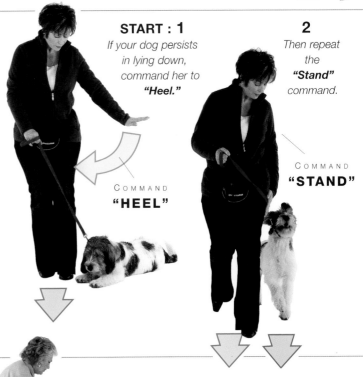

START : 1
If your dog persists in lying down, command her to **"Heel."**

COMMAND **"HEEL"**

2
Then repeat the **"Stand"** *command.*

COMMAND **"STAND"**

TIME TRAINING

Left: *Once a dog will stand consistently for you, it's time to move away a little and practice a Stand/Stay at a distance. But keep the exercises quite short — 10 seconds is fine to start with, and 30 seconds a suggested maximum.*

10 seconds
20 seconds
30 seconds

Left: *When you want to practice Stand/Stay exercises, first call your dog over to you and put it in a stand.*

Retrieve games with a favorite toy go over well.

An outstretched arm signifies **"Stand."**

Above: *Finish off your training with a game that will allow the dog to burn off some of its excess energy. Stand/Stays do not come naturally to many dogs so you must reward a solid performance.*

TEACHING THE DOWN

Dogs that will lie obediently in the down position — particularly when there are distractions around — are a genuine pleasure to be with.

The Down Position

The Down is in my view the most useful training a dog can learn. It has many uses — you may be chatting for some time in the street with a friend, or perhaps you are standing in line and your dog needs to lie down to be out of the way. It also helps to teach the dog to lie in the corner of a room or on its bed when guests arrive. It's also a comfortable position for a dog to be in.

The down/stay position can also help to control and calm excitable dogs. Once a dog has learned the rewards connected with the Down, they love performing it.

The Down Using Food (puppy safe)

In the house and garden get your dog into the sit position, as it is easiest to train a dog to lie down from the Sit. When the dog is sitting, extend a small treat like a piece of ham or cheese toward its nose with your right hand. As the dog stretches forward to take

the food, drop your right hand down to the floor enticing the dog's nose to follow suit. This naturally encourages the dog to slide downward into the Down — as the dog lies down obediently, give it the tidbit while simultaneously commanding **"Down"** in a crisp tone of voice. Then verbally praise **"Good dog"** — remember that praise should be given in a whisper. Many owners forget to change their tone and the dogs only hear an indecipherable monotone throughout the lesson, which slows the training process. This should be repeated several times.

The Down Using a Toy (puppy safe)

You can achieve the same results using a toy instead of a food tidbit. It helps to add variety to see what will work best for you and your dog. Once the toy has been placed on the floor and the dog has slid down to meet it, hold the toy in place for a few seconds and then throw it for a retrieve. Alternatively command your dog to **"Sit"** first, then, placing the toy near its nose, command **"Down"** and lower the toy to the ground. The dog should slide into the down position and you should praise it enthusiastically. Pause, heel forward slightly then repeat the exercise again.

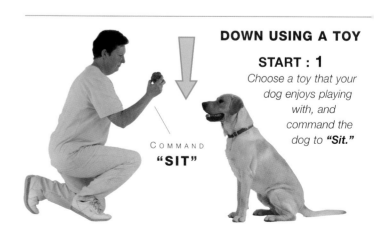

DOWN USING A TOY

START : 1
Choose a toy that your dog enjoys playing with, and command the dog to "Sit."

COMMAND
"SIT"

DOWN USING FOOD

START : 1
Use a small tidbit of food to attract your dog's attention.

COMMAND
"DOWN"

2
As the dog stretches its muzzle forward to take the offered treat, just draw your hand back a little and encourage it to follow the tidbit down to the floor.

4
Now make a fuss over her — she's done well!

PRAISE
"GOOD GIRL"

3
The downward motion in conjunction with the stretch toward the tidbit should cause the dog to slide into the down position. Give it the treat.

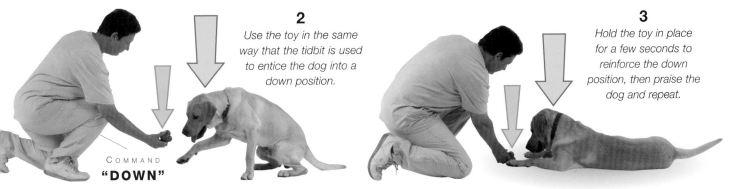

2
Use the toy in the same way that the tidbit is used to entice the dog into a down position.

COMMAND
"DOWN"

3
Hold the toy in place for a few seconds to reinforce the down position, then praise the dog and repeat.

TEACHING THE DOWN

START : 1

For extra control, particularly when training large dogs around the house, it's a good idea to use a collar and leash. But don't simply use the leash as a way of dragging the dog into the Down. Tempt it down with a tidbit or toy.

3

While the dog is in the down position, put your foot on the leash about 30 cm (12 in.) from its neck. If the dog tries to sit up now, the leash will tighten and hold it back.

DOWN USING A COLLAR AND LEAD

C O M M A N D
"DOWN"

2

*As the dog sinks down in response to the food lure, give the **"Down"** command.*

The Down Using a Collar and Leash (puppy safe)

Some owners find that it is more practical to use a collar and leash for all the exercises in the home or that their dog is much calmer when on a leash. This is fine — simply repeat the food or toy method only the dog is now leashed. When your dog is lying down, place your foot on the leash about 30 cm (12 in.) from the dog's neck. Please remember that the leash must be loose and should not tighten when you place your foot on it. If it does, lift your foot for a second and let

the dog get more comfortable; when the leash is loose, place your foot on it again. If the dog now decides to sit up, the leash will inhibit the upward action while simultaneously you will command **"Down."** This works with many dogs to prevent their upward movement. Never drag the dog down. If the dog's rear end rises as it's about to get up, press down on the rump quickly before the dog has gotten up. Otherwise begin again. Don't get involved in a physical trial of strength, as this will disorient the dog and cause some panic. Use the leash cautiously.

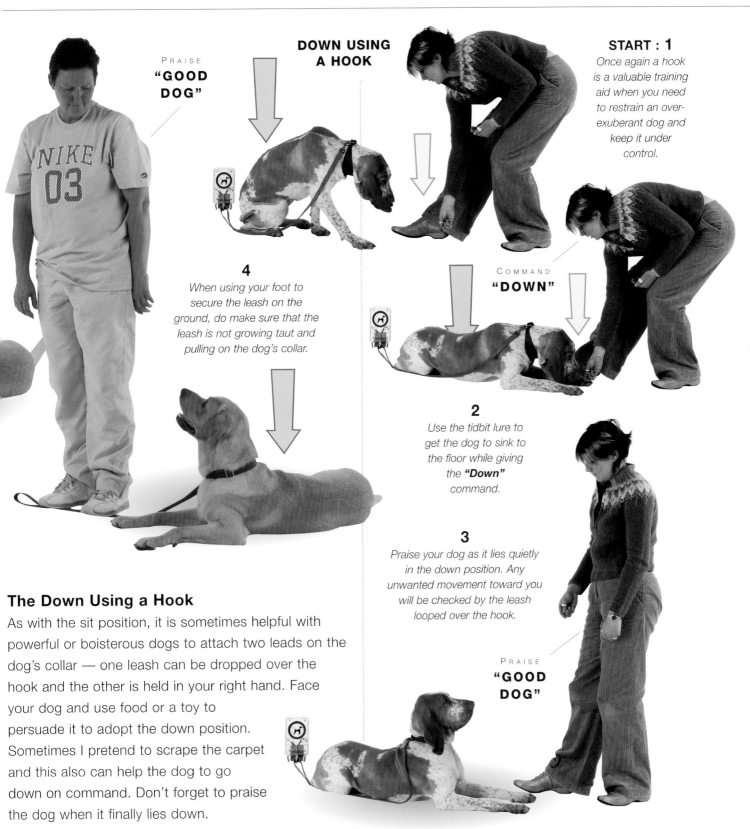

PRAISE
"GOOD DOG"

DOWN USING A HOOK

START : 1

Once again a hook is a valuable training aid when you need to restrain an over-exuberant dog and keep it under control.

4

When using your foot to secure the leash on the ground, do make sure that the leash is not growing taut and pulling on the dog's collar.

COMMAND
"DOWN"

2

*Use the tidbit lure to get the dog to sink to the floor while giving the **"Down"** command.*

3

Praise your dog as it lies quietly in the down position. Any unwanted movement toward you will be checked by the leash looped over the hook.

PRAISE
"GOOD DOG"

The Down Using a Hook

As with the sit position, it is sometimes helpful with powerful or boisterous dogs to attach two leads on the dog's collar — one leash can be dropped over the hook and the other is held in your right hand. Face your dog and use food or a toy to persuade it to adopt the down position. Sometimes I pretend to scrape the carpet and this also can help the dog to go down on command. Don't forget to praise the dog when it finally lies down.

DOWNS AND DOWN/STAYS

The Down Using a Push (puppy safe)

This is especially good for less dominant types of dog. Place your dog on your left side attached to the leash and collar. Stand still and command the dog to **"Sit"** at your left side. Once sitting, press on the dog's back behind its shoulder blades, saying **"Down."** As you do so, gently pull the leash in a downward motion to the floor — the two guiding actions encourage the dog to lie down. Dutifully praise the dog when it's done. Some dogs react against this push and pull method, but not many. If your dog reacts by struggling, choose another training style. Remember to be firm yet gentle; you are guiding the dog downward, not using brute force. If you yank the leash down and push roughly on the dog's back, you may induce a sense of panic.

Down/Stay

The technique explained in the Sit/Stay (see pages 94–99) is also used to teach the Down/Stay. You work incrementally, building up

the time that you command your dog to stay in the down position and the distance you walk to separate yourself from the dog. As the Down is a comfortable position for a dog, you may build up to longer duration stays, eventually reaching three minutes as described in the 21-Day Training Program.

Location Training

Training dogs can be frustrating at times because we often assume that dogs think like us, or at least see the world as we do. Well, they don't. Nothing demonstrates better how dogs actually learn than location training. By this I mean teaching the dog to carry out all its learned training in any location you choose. This will involve two unpredictable factors: the different location and all the distractions that may be present. Dogs that will happily obey your commands willingly in the house often don't appear to even understand the

The boxer remains admirably in the down position despite the border collies tearing around in the background.

Do remember that dog training is not an end in itself — it has a practical purpose. You want your dog to obey you at all times and in all locations. So make sure that you practice in the park where there are lots of distractions around.

DOWN USING A PUSH

START : 1

When training using the Down with a Push method, begin with the dog on the leash and sitting by your side.

2

*Command **"Down"** and simultaneously push the dog between its shoulder blades while drawing it downward with the leash.*

3

When the dog assumes the down position correctly, praise it for getting it right. Take care with the amount of physical coercion that you use in this exercise — you must be firm but not insensitive or rough with the dog. If it starts to panic, you'll get nowhere.

COMMAND
"DOWN"

PRAISE
"GOOD DOG"

basic **"Sit"** command when in another location.

Once trained to a basic level, dogs really need to practice all the exercises in as many different places as you can find. The more distractions they can overcome or become accustomed to, the more steady the training becomes. Of course, the outside world offers plenty of distractions, perhaps in the form of other canines, cats racing along sidewalks and across the road, traffic noises or people passing by. The outside world is full of fascinating scents that excite the dog's most powerful sensory faculty. It's a recipe that can cause havoc with concentration.

Even if you are only training your dog to a fairly basic level of obedience, it still has to learn to be obedient in parks, shopping malls and other public places. Your dog needs to learn to obey your

commands while other dogs are around. In the urban jungle of busy shopping streets a dog cannot be allowe to cut across pedestrians or pull away to sniff at any other dog they may see. In teaching dogs not to do what their instincts tell them it is natural to do, we turn their world upside down, but that is the price of having them as pets in our complex society.

Once a dog obeys all your commands reliably, then the motivational inducements — such as food, a toy or touch — are removed. You merely make a command, such as **"Sit,"** and the dog is verbally praised when it obeys. That's it. Occasionally the odd toy or tidbit can be produced as reinforcement; however, all trained dogs should obey your commands with your verbal praise as their sole reward.

WEEK 2 TRAINING

START : 1

Dogs may get overexcited when you attach the leash in anticipation of a walk. That's when you must avoid undignified tussles like this – remember your training!

2

The leader goes through the front door first. If your dog tries to push ahead of you, pull the door shut in its face.

Sit/Stand/Down/Stay Training — Week 2

At least 63 lessons (three times three lessons for seven days) should have been completed by the end of the first week for each discipline. Check that your dog is obeying your commands in most of the circumstances described previously. Some owners will progress faster than others and this is determined by factors like the dog's breed, its age, your skills and how many bad habits the dog has learned before beginning this course.

Entering the Real World

Though most people want an obedient dog in the home, their main concern is how to control their dog in the outside world. Of course an obedient dog that has continual training and doesn't try to dominate every visitor who enters the house is a controlled dog, and is much more likely to listen to you when outside the home.

It is now time to transfer the majority of your training lessons to the outside world and to practice in many of the locations in which your dog needs to be obedient. For my examples I'll use the local park, but your area for training may be different. For safety, especially with dogs that may run off when released, it is best to get well into the park — at least 200 m (600 ft.) from the entrance — so that if anything goes wrong your dog is well away from any road traffic.

You may be training in remote fields or on land where few dogs are likely to appear. This is fine for a few days, but the reality is that the more you train in situations where your dog is likely to be distracted and you overcome this through your power as a leader and trainer, the higher standard of training you will achieve. At times your willpower will be tested, as your dog struggles to give in to its innate drives to investigate other dogs and its surroundings. If your dog has already learned bad habits such as chasing bicycles,

3

That's more like it. You go through the door first and then instruct the dog to "Come" when you are ready for it to follow you.

4

Now you can make your way to the park in a controlled manner. If your dog pulls or lags behind, remember the lessons you learned in the Heelwork chapter and put them into practice.

pestering pedestrians or other people with dogs who wish to be left alone, then these ingrained behaviors will test you and your dog many times before you get the balance of control right.

Training in Action — The Walk to the Park

Dogs often become excited, even overexcited, as you prepare for a walk from the house to the park. It is normal fun for the dog, but if that excitement interrupts you trying to leave the house in an orderly fashion, it is defeating the exercise for all concerned. We need routine and order, and the dog must learn this step by step. Here are a few practical scenarios to help you put your dog's training to good use.

First, connect the leash to your dog in the house. If the dog accepts this with general enthusiasm, that's fine. If it becomes so overexcited that even connecting the leash becomes a trial, then confuse the animal by making three or four false starts. Sit down after each

one and eventually the dog will calm down as it will no longer know when you really mean to walk. Once you're ready to exit the house, remember that the dog must not be allowed to barge ahead of you through the front door.

You should have already been training the dog around your home in the first week to wait at doors while you walk through first. Your dog should now be waiting for you to take the lead. Leave the house and slam the door in the dog's face even if it tries to take the lead just once (see the Leadership Program in Chapter 3). I know all of this takes time, but the end result is an orderly exit with no slammed doors, no shouting and no pulling for dear life.

If you have a front yard gate, repeat the whole process here too — you go first, your dog waits. Remember that the dog is learning to link each action and command with a reward. Don't forget to praise the dog each and every time it does what you want.

THE WALK TO THE PARK

Take a walk down the street. Now the distractions appear, and if the dog begins to surge ahead, all that heel training involving left turns, right turns and about turns comes into play. Don't let the dog stop for sniffs or to say hello to another dog, just keep walking briskly. For some dogs this will seem like very hard work at first, and in that case there is no harm in simply walking for a few blocks and then going back to the house if you are tired or feel the dog is getting the upper hand. It's no use losing your leadership edge. However, with most dogs, you can continue to the park.

This experience is teaching your dog that no matter how eager it is to go for a walk, you have the right to change direction whenever you wish and you will do so if it begins to pull. Don't forget to snap the leash if the dog tries to pull you into a hedge or veer off for a sniff. Executing an about turn does wonders for a dog's concentration as you pivot on your left foot swinging around with your right knee and virtually walking into the dog. Off you go again, encouraging the dog to stay by your left side and praising it when it does so. Other pedestrians might think this odd, but that's beside the point.

Practicing the Sit and maybe the Down will help to steady the dog. If it expects that you may say **"Sit"** every few hundred feet, it will start to pay more attention to you in anticipation of receiving a piece of ham when it's near your left side or when it turns about on cue with you. The less the dog predicts your behavior, the more it has to listen to you.

If you have implemented the Leadership Program described in Chapter 3, this too will increase your dog's desire to watch and listen to you, which makes for faster training. As the dog learns what you want, the rewards increase and the corrections diminish.

At the Park — Find Your Training Area

It's now time to practice all the lessons you have been teaching your dog in this new arena, ideally with as few distractions as possible while the dog gets used to being trained in the park.

- **The Sit**
- **The Stand**
- **The Down**
- **The Heel**
- **The Sit/Stay on or off the leash**
- **The Stand/Stay on or off the leash**
- **The Down/Stay on or off the leash**
- **The Recall**
- **Finish with a controlled play period**

3
Vary your turns as you go.

2
While the dog is walking calmly to heel, praise it and command ***"Heel"*** *as you execute a turn.*

COMMAND
"HEEL"

PRAISE
"GOOD DOG"

6

Use your knee to nudge the dog into a left turn if it loses concentration. By throwing in unpredictable turns and sits, and rewarding obedience with praise and the odd tidbit, you remain the focus of attention.

4

*Every now and then ask the dog to **"Sit."** It'll be more on its toes if it doesn't know quite what to expect.*

COMMAND
"SIT"

5

Give some quiet words of praise when the dog watches you attentively.

COMMAND
"HEEL"

MAINTAINING CONTROL

The walk to the park will expose your dog to all the multifarious delights and distractions that the outside world has to offer. There are new scents to sniff, new people and dogs to greet, new places to explore. This is when your training is put to the test and you will need to employ all the heelwork skills described in Chapter 8.

COMMAND
"HEEL"

PRAISE
"GOOD DOG"

START : 1

Once you are outside the front gate — you went through it first, I hope — get your dog nicely positioned on your left-hand side and then heel off down the street.

SIT/STAYS IN THE PARK

The Sit/Stay — Signal and Time

The next stage is to teach your dog to remain obedient to the **"Stay"** command in the park while increasing the distance of separation to the full length of the leash and incorporating hand signals. Make your dog sit on your left-hand side. As you leave the dog, hold the flat of your hand a short distance in front of the dog's face and command **"Stay"** simultaneously.

Now walk away from the dog keeping your eye on it the entire time. Turn and face the dog when you are about 1 m (3 ft.) away. Wait about five seconds. If the dog does not move, return to it either by walking around the dog counterclockwise or by retracing your route. Varying the return helps reinforce the Stay. Once the exercise is complete, give your dog lots of praise. Only use food rewards if they don't overexcite the dog. Some dogs concentrate too much on the food and not enough on what's being said. I tend to use food sparingly — if at all — for the Stay.

Common Sit/Stay Problems
The dog keeps following me
Solution: The dog is probably confused — check that your own training actions are correct. Go back to moving just one step away from the dog until its stability improves.

This exercise builds on the Sit/Stay method you were introduced to on pages 94–99 — you are now accustoming your dog to a Stay while it is exposed to distractions in the outside world.

COMMAND
"STAY"

START : 1
*Give a verbal **"Stay"** command, and back it up by holding the flat of your hand in front of the dog's face. Prepare to walk away.*

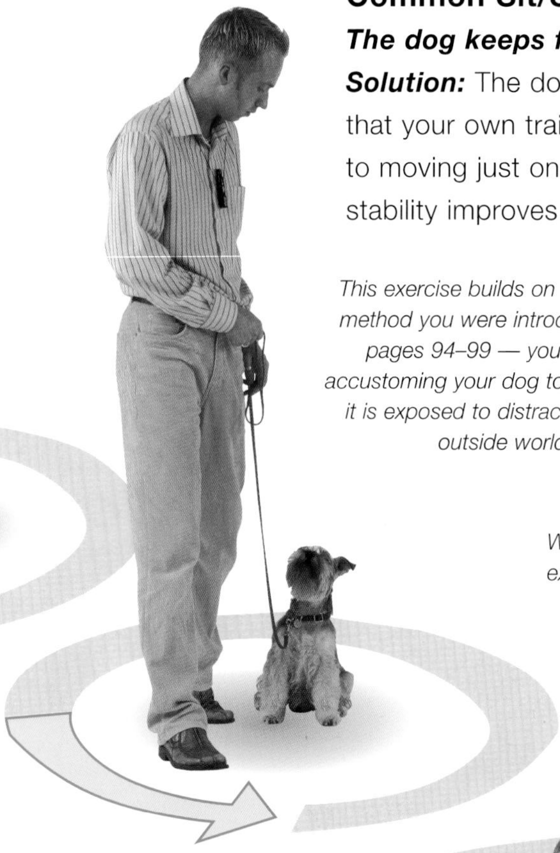

2
Step away from the sitting dog, allowing the leash to play out behind you.

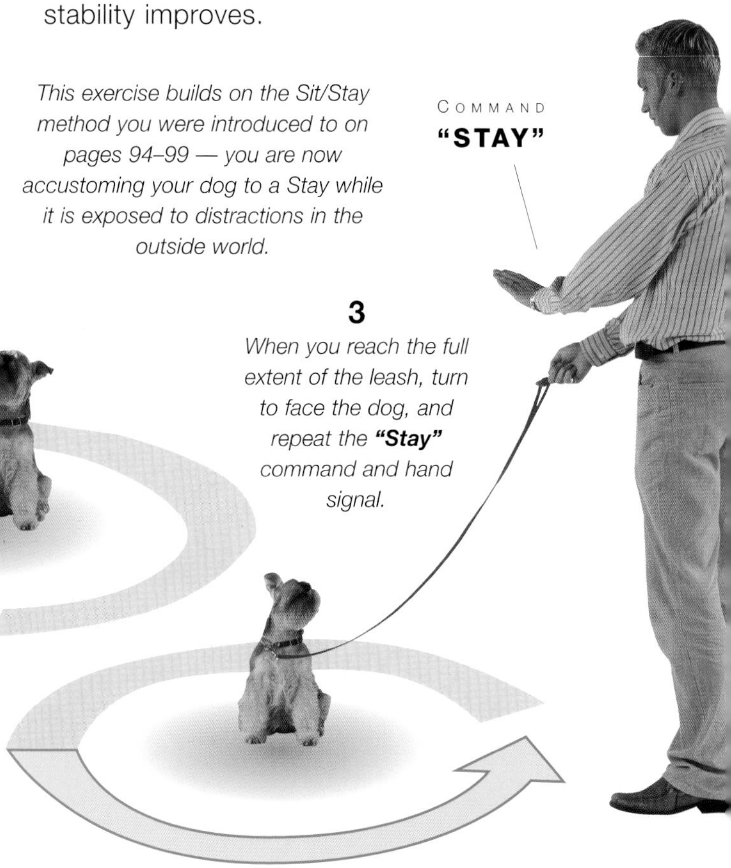

COMMAND
"STAY"

3
*When you reach the full extent of the leash, turn to face the dog, and repeat the **"Stay"** command and hand signal.*

The dog moves when I turn and face it
Solution:

- Are you slightly tugging the leash?
- Are you remembering to use the hand signal?
- Are you anticipating the move and re-commanding the dog to **"Stay"** firmly before it actually moves?

The dog moves upon my return and gets excited
Solution: With excitable dogs, tone down your words of praise upon your return, and wait a few seconds at the dog's side before praising it. Re-commanding **"Stay"** as you stand next to your dog helps to stabilize it.

Don't despair if things go wrong from time to time and your dog moves out of the sit/stay. Check that you are not confusing the dog by sending out mixed signals, or getting it too excited when you praise it. It pays to go back to square one and reestablish stability at just a single pace away.

PRAISE
"GOOD DOG"

Take care not to tug on the leash while you are stepping away from and returning to your dog. You don't want to unsettle it while you are trying to cement the sit/stay.

4
Keep the dog in the stay position for a few seconds before starting to walk back to it in a counterclockwise direction.

5
Continue around behind the dog and then return to your start position with the dog seated on your left.

6
The dog has remained sitting still throughout the exercise and despite the competing attractions of all the things going on around it in the park. It certainly deserves some warm words of praise.

PRACTICING THE STAYS

Stay Positions — Time and Distance Training

Next, you are going to extend the use of the stay positions while location training in an environment where your dog will experience outside distractions. This normally takes place during Week 2 of the program, although some dogs do learn quicker than others.

Time is the most crucial part of the Stay. If your dog will eventually lie down for a full five minutes while you stand about 3 m (9 ft.) away from it, and will do that consistently, then that dog has achieved a great deal and the training will be rock solid for future use. Strangely, once the basic stay position has been learned, most owners seem to want to see how far they can walk away from their dog or want to call their dog from this distance to them. Both actions undermine the training at a very delicate stage, and really confuse the dog.

Next, begin to drop the leash as you walk off to stand no further than about 2 m (6 ft.) from the dog. Also begin to increase the time you leave the dog in the sit position, for instance, up to about one minute. If the dog attempts to move, command **"Stay"** again. If the dog moves toward you, always go back to the dog and very quickly place it in exactly the same position that it left, not the place where you caught it. Dogs know where they were placed and can quickly learn to get near you, which is a natural desire. When a dog will stay in sit/stay position for one minute, and you are able to return and praise it, say three times per lesson without error, then you're making good progress.

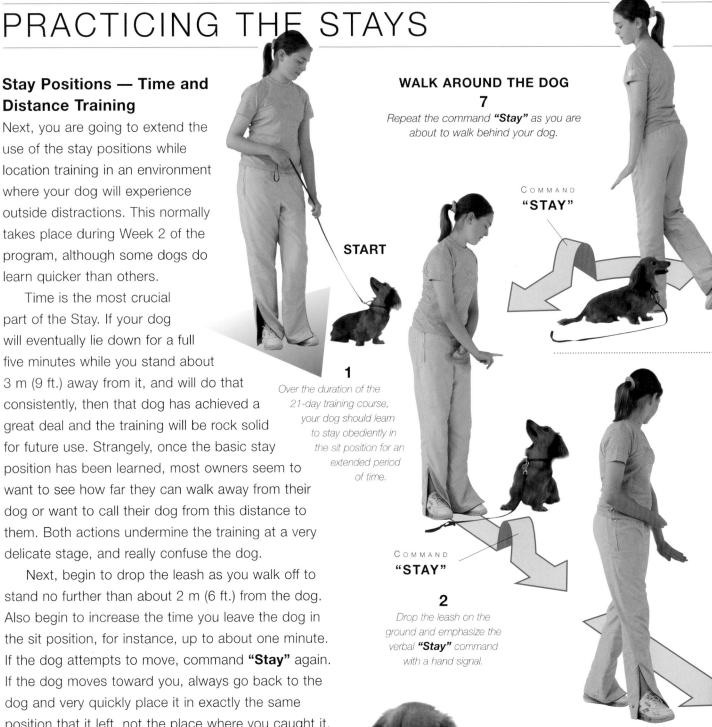

START

1

Over the duration of the 21-day training course, your dog should learn to stay obediently in the sit position for an extended period of time.

C O M M A N D
"STAY"

2

*Drop the leash on the ground and emphasize the verbal **"Stay"** command with a hand signal.*

WALK AROUND THE DOG
7

*Repeat the command **"Stay"** as you are about to walk behind your dog.*

C O M M A N D
"STAY"

OUTWARD
3

*As you walk off to a distance of about three meters (nine feet) from your dog, make sure that its attention does not wander. Repeat the **"Stay"** command if necessary, and use a hand signal as a means of visual reinforcement.*

8

nce back in the start position, ut your left foot on the leash.

9

Pick up the leash. Note how this dog is closely attentive to its handler and has not moved even during the tricky period when she moved out of sight behind it.

10

The dog certainly deserves plenty of praise and the occasional tidbit for performing the Sit/Stay so well.

RETURN

6

Make the return quite brisk and deliberate. If you dawdle back, you risk the dog becoming impatient and giving in to the temptation of coming to meet you.

5

Once the dog has demonstrated that it will sit obediently for an extended period, you can walk back to it. If it moves during the Sit/Stay, go back and return it to its original position.

COMMAND
"STAY"

Again a clear hand signal backs up the verbal command.

4

*At the furthest point from the dog, turn to face it and reiterate the **"Stay"** command. You want the dog to remain in this position initially for a minute.*

COMMAND
"STAY"

PRACTICING THE STAYS

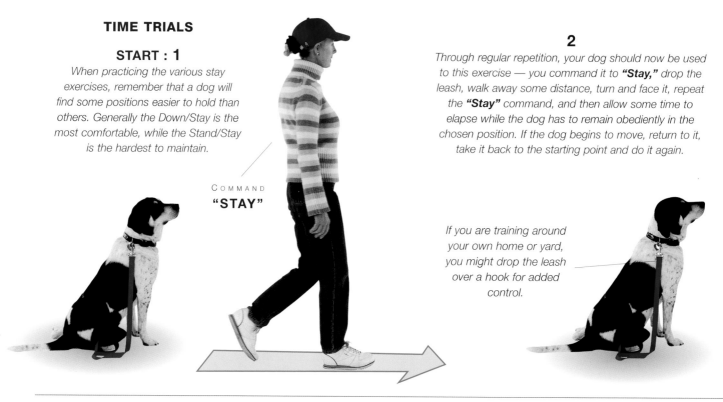

TIME TRIALS

START : 1

When practicing the various stay exercises, remember that a dog will find some positions easier to hold than others. Generally the Down/Stay is the most comfortable, while the Stand/Stay is the hardest to maintain.

COMMAND
"STAY"

2

*Through regular repetition, your dog should now be used to this exercise — you command it to **"Stay,"** drop the leash, walk away some distance, turn and face it, repeat the **"Stay"** command, and then allow some time to elapse while the dog has to remain obediently in the chosen position. If the dog begins to move, return to it, take it back to the starting point and do it again.*

If you are training around your own home or yard, you might drop the leash over a hook for added control.

How Long Should I Maintain Stay Positions?

During the first week, most dogs can be left in the sit and down/stay positions for up to a minute before you return. The Stand may take a week longer as dogs find it easier to move toward you from the Stand.

The Sit/Stay by the end of Week 2 or 3 can be extended to two minutes and 2 m (6 ft.) distance not holding the leash. The Down/Stay by the end of Week 2 should be reaching about two minutes duration and maybe a distance of 5 m (15 ft.) or so. In this training the Stand/Stay will not exceed one minute in duration for reasons of comfort. The Sit/Stay should reach about two minutes maximum and the Down/Stay about three minutes maximum during Week 3.

Training Tips

Remember to have some hooks positioned at strategic places in the house or yard that you can drop the end of the leash over before you tell your dog to sit/, stand/ or down/stay. If the dog begins to move or follow you, it is automatically restrained by the leash; if you simultaneously re-command **"Stay"** the dogs often associate the restraint with your command and this again helps. If the dog has moved position, always return to it and start again.

If your dog is moving more than it is staying, which means that it is receiving more correction than praise, simply switch exercises and do something the dog can achieve well and leave that particular exercise until the next training schedule or a little later in the current training period. **Don't ever repeat training that upsets or confuses the dog.** It slows down training and takes away any sense of fun.

If the dog seems lethargic and uninterested, try distracting it with a quick ball or squeaky toy game for a minute or two and then return to the training. Once the entire training lesson is complete, always play

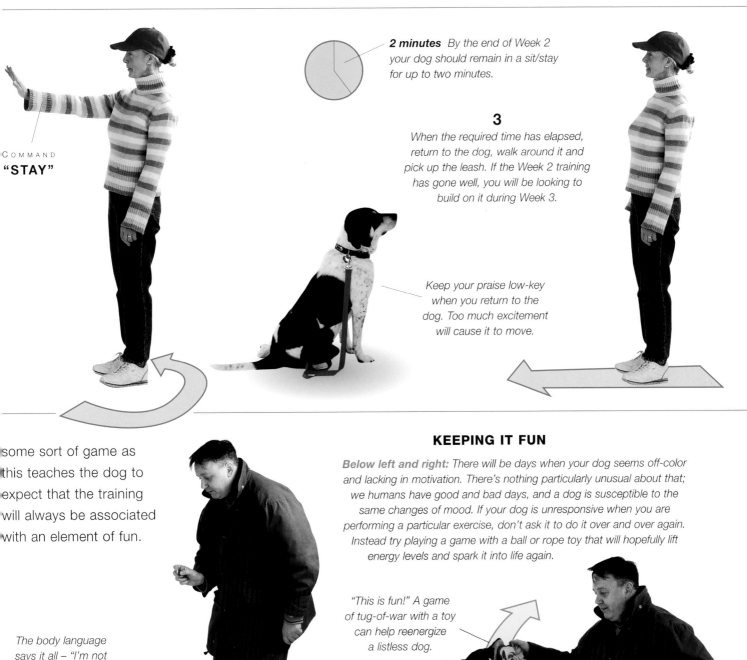

COMMAND
"STAY"

2 minutes By the end of Week 2 your dog should remain in a sit/stay for up to two minutes.

3

When the required time has elapsed, return to the dog, walk around it and pick up the leash. If the Week 2 training has gone well, you will be looking to build on it during Week 3.

Keep your praise low-key when you return to the dog. Too much excitement will cause it to move.

some sort of game as this teaches the dog to expect that the training will always be associated with an element of fun.

KEEPING IT FUN

Below left and right: There will be days when your dog seems off-color and lacking in motivation. There's nothing particularly unusual about that; we humans have good and bad days, and a dog is susceptible to the same changes of mood. If your dog is unresponsive when you are performing a particular exercise, don't ask it to do it over and over again. Instead try playing a game with a ball or rope toy that will hopefully lift energy levels and spark it into life again.

"This is fun!" A game of tug-of-war with a toy can help reenergize a listless dog.

The body language says it all – "I'm not interested".

INTO WEEK 3

The Stays — Week 3

By the end of Week 3, the Stays should be progressing well. Though you will still be carrying out some training in and around the home throughout the day, the outside training places should be the main focus now. Bear in mind that if you are doing well, then the Down/Stay can be prolonged up to about five minutes without the dog moving once.

This is when I start to get friends to walk their dog on a leash about 10 m (30 ft.) in length around my dog when it is in a down/stay in the park or yard. Even though my dog may be staying happily at a distance of 5 m (15 ft.) in the house, I tend initially to move away no further than 1 m (3 ft.) from the dog when introducing the dog decoy distraction in the park. If your dog moves, command **"Stay"** in a sharp admonishing voice. Maybe hold the leash for the first few practices. If your dog lunges at the other dog, snap the leash sharply and say **"Sit/Stay."** The idea is that you only begin to leave your dog in the Sit/ or Down/Stay and walk a full two meters (six feet) away when it is steady and does not move in reaction to the other dog. Remember, your dog needs to learn that "Stay" means "Stay" everywhere, and that is what you are training.

Some dogs stay with no problem whatsoever even when the distractions are introduced. Different distractions affect different dogs in different ways. Whatever your dog's weakness, practice the stays while always bearing in mind that you should not place yourself and your dog in a position where you might lose control and let the dog get its own way. Patience is a must, and with regular practice I find that all dogs eventually follow your commands.

Common Problems in the Park or Street

Other people come up and encourage your dog to jump up or take its attention from you.

Solution: Explain that you are training and your dog must not be allowed to use them as reason to misbehave. Tell them they can stroke your dog only if it sits and for a short time.

If other dog owners seem unable to control their willful pets, ask them politely to control their dogs. If this does not help, move to another area of the park.

Your park has many stray animals or dogs around.

Solution: Take a friend who can help you to achieve your training program and keep unwanted animals away.

Below: When you practice stays in the park, be prepared for your dog to react to various distractions like other dogs, people walking past, joggers, etc. You will need to be patient and it makes sense to use a leash initially so that you retain control at all times.

New dogs to greet on every side — this is harder than training in the privacy of your own yard.

THE **STAY** POSITIONS

INTRODUCING DISTRACTIONS

START : 1
When the stays seem to be well embedded, you should ask a friend to walk her dog nearby while you are training to provide a distraction.

2
When you start to introduce this distraction, stand a bit closer to your dog than you have done previously. You can work on or off the leash – it's your call.

COMMAND
"STAY"

4
It helps if the "decoy" dog is well trained also.

3
With practice you can increase the number of circuits that the "decoy" dog makes.

Fun and Games

After your training session is complete, do play some fun games with your dog as opposed to simply letting it wander off to find its own amusement. Remember as a leader you need to lead and be a central part of your dog's walk. This does not mean your dog can't play with other dogs, but not while training is in progress. If your dog is particularly dog-focused, limit its access to other canine company until the training has achieved the desired level of obedience.

Going Home

Many people gleefully tell me that their dogs are much better behaved on the way home. Of course, they are like children at the end of an exciting day — they are tired. This does not mean that they are necessarily more obedient, although this can appear to be the case. Carry on with your training but do allow for a little more listlessness as opposed to disobedience.

CHAPTER TEN

The Recall

Teaching your dog to come to you on command in any location is very important for safety and control. This chapter will show you many ways to achieve this. These training techniques work for most dogs. So if you have not yet trained your dog to come to you when called, read on and select the training method you think best suits your dog and circumstances.

Many people reading this book will have a dog that has proved difficult to train, but the training methods I offer suit these dogs as well. Provided that you understand what and how your dog learns, the dog will be able to do the rest with your guidance.

Why Won't My Dog Come?

Why do so many people have a problem with getting their dogs to come back to them, and why do some dogs cannily learn to give their owners the runaround? The following reasons are normally the cause. First, the dog may have been punished physically or verbally by an owner who believes that the dog will retrospectively associate his present anger and the punishment with its reluctance to come to him. Well, the dog cannot make this association and this type of reaction simply destroys the dog's confidence in you. Even if you have to catch the dog, punishing it will simply cause it to associate the action of you grabbing it with an unpleasant experience.

The Disinterested Owner

This type of owner is the one who takes a dog out when young and sets it free to more or less discover its own routines. He or she likes to watch it play with other dogs, which a casual observer might believe is quite normal. Unfortunately many dogs will come to regard their supposed leader as merely a pack member, and not one to be listened to. And when a dog does not listen, it is difficult to get its attention for recall training when needed. Would you take an interest in someone who ignores you for an hour a day on a walk?

These owners find it hard to attract the dog, which has now discovered the fun of chasing other dogs. The dog does not see them as fun or interesting to be with. And just because they want to go home, why should the dog concern itself? These owners then devise ways of catching their dog — often asking others to take hold of its collar for them while the dog learns to

It is not easy to gain your dog's attention when it is playing.

PAY ATTENTION!

If a dog fails to come back when called, part of the problem may lie with the owner. A disinterested handler who lets a dog romp around unsupervised in the park may be storing up trouble for himself.

counter these actions in turn. Stalemate. If you fit this category, I can help realign you and your dog. When you learn to be a leader, the dog will learn to listen.

Delayed Training

Many dog owners get ill-informed advice from people who say that dogs should not be trained until they've grown up a little and had their puppyhood. Unfortunately, this is the most crucial time of learning. Some of you will appreciate this if you inherit an untrained rescue dog. I train all my puppies from 6 weeks for obedience and especially recall. Their natural desire to stay near you helps this training, so don't waste that instinct. Don't be complacent about this situation. As the pup grows, the distance it is prepared to run off from its owner generally increases, its confidence grows and slowly the owner realizes they have a problem on their hands. Try to avoid this — train from day one.

The retriever shows some ritualized aggressive threats to put the young upstart in its place.

Socializing with other dogs helps a puppy to find its place in the world, but don't let it have it all its own way and ignore training during this formative period. Here the puppy is focused on the other dog — the owner is not on its mind.

This Akita puppy is being left to its own devices as it seeks to socialize with an adult golden retriever who is not keen on its advances.

PUPPY TRAINING

The Dog's Natural Drives

A dog is born with a number of innate drives that help it to survive in the wild like its cousin, the wolf. As a puppy it begins to explore both the natural world and the unnatural domestic world that we occupy. It explores all the exotic smells in its environment, it plays with and investigates the other dogs it meets, and observes everything that is happening nearby. While it is experiencing these natural pleasures, you are often the last thing on your dog's mind, unless you have already begun training and forming a strong bond with the dog in these same places. However much you train, the dog still has ample time to enjoy being a dog at home and the park.

Once a dog has found out how to occupy itself, it tends to form its own little routines. That's fine provided you can interrupt them when necessary. You may wish to call the dog away from a person whom the dog is trying to greet but who does not relish this sort of attention. When you call your dog, its obedience simply depends on whether the motivation to obey you outweighs what the dog is focused on at that moment. Here is the crux of the problem. We love watching our dogs galloping across the park and running and chasing other dogs. It's a lovely, natural sight. The socialization aspect of these encounters is also crucial to your dog forming positive attitudes to dogs and people and its environment. In other words, it prepares your dog for life in our world, but it has to obey certain rules to survive in that same world. This is what we call training.

Most dogs like retrieving, and this willingness to retrieve can be

Right: A puppy's growth to maturity is a journey of exploration in which it is learning about and responding to the world all around it.

now improved, shaped and used to help with the Recall and other exercises during our training program. I will outline several types of training approaches to alter your dog's behavior. Select the one that fits your dog's personality best. Sometimes a combination of one or more methods also quickens the learning process for your dog.

Puppy Recall

If you have a young puppy and wish to start off on the right foot, this is an ideal time to start training. Puppies have a natural instinct to stay by the pack and especially near to the leader(s). The leader is — or should be — you. If you apply some natural dog training psychology allied to an understanding of what the puppy's innate instincts are, then teaching the Retrieve should be much easier. Moreover, if you build up a hands-on relationship

Recall Problems — Causes in Brief

- Owners choose a breed that is too difficult to own and train for their level. of experience.

- Owners delay training a puppy and miss out on a crucial learning period.

- Owners have allowed their dog to retain its own pleasures from puppyhood.

- Owners do not train recall in all situations, including the home, from the time the puppy is six weeks old.

- Owners do not take on the Alpha (leader) role immediately.

- Owners do not train the puppy daily to come in all situations.

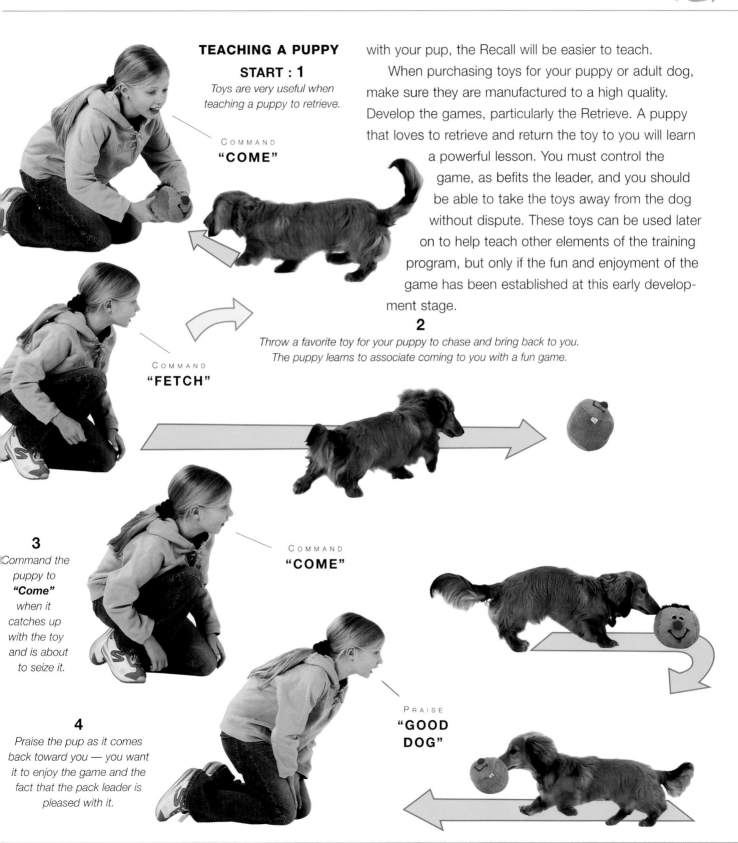

TEACHING A PUPPY

START : 1

Toys are very useful when teaching a puppy to retrieve.

COMMAND
"COME"

with your pup, the Recall will be easier to teach.

When purchasing toys for your puppy or adult dog, make sure they are manufactured to a high quality. Develop the games, particularly the Retrieve. A puppy that loves to retrieve and return the toy to you will learn a powerful lesson. You must control the game, as befits the leader, and you should be able to take the toys away from the dog without dispute. These toys can be used later on to help teach other elements of the training program, but only if the fun and enjoyment of the game has been established at this early development stage.

2

Throw a favorite toy for your puppy to chase and bring back to you. The puppy learns to associate coming to you with a fun game.

COMMAND
"FETCH"

3

Command the puppy to **"Come"** when it catches up with the toy and is about to seize it.

COMMAND
"COME"

4

Praise the pup as it comes back toward you — you want it to enjoy the game and the fact that the pack leader is pleased with it.

PRAISE
"GOOD DOG"

RECALL WITH A TOY

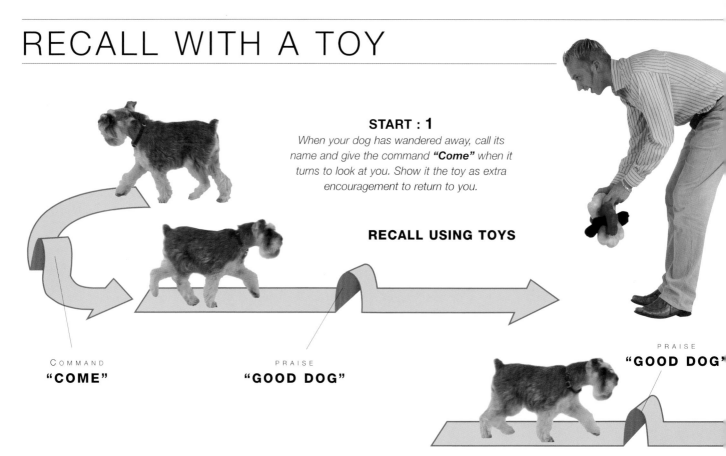

START : 1

*When your dog has wandered away, call its name and give the command **"Come"** when it turns to look at you. Show it the toy as extra encouragement to return to you.*

RECALL USING TOYS

COMMAND
"COME"

PRAISE
"GOOD DOG"

PRAISE
"GOOD DOG"

Recall with a Toy (puppy safe)

Assuming your dog loves fetching its toys, begin by selecting the two identical toys that it likes most. For some dogs this can be an old piece of rope or a favorite squeaky toy that mimics the sound of prey. Oddly enough, to help speed up training lock all the toys away in a box except these two. Why? So that when you show the dog its toy, it really becomes excited at the sight and thought of the game to come. You may be using the toy to teach the Recall, but the dog imagines no such thing. It sees the toy and remembers the fun it had last time you played together. You need to focus the dog's attention on you through the toy and make the link of recall training.

Begin by hiding the squeaky toy on you, then wander around the house or yard. It is a good idea to use this exercise to break up the others like the Sit, Stand and Down. Variety helps to keep your dog's attention focused. When your dog has wandered off, call its name sharply, pause and give the command

"Come" when it looks around. Show the toy, wave it in the air and/or squeak it. As your dog begins to run for the reward, praise it verbally. (It is crucial always to praise a dog while it is on its way to you and not just when it arrives.) As soon as the dog arrives at your feet, throw the toy for a Retrieve — don't tell the dog to sit, just throw the toy. If it brings the toy back, take the toy and give your dog plenty of praise.

2

Praise the dog verbally as it hurries back toward you and the enticing prospect of a game with the toy.

3

Praise the dog again when it ends up dutifully at your feet. Your encouragement helps to motivate your dog to obey.

PRAISE WHERE PRAISE IS DUE

Dogs love to be praised by their "pack leader" so try to keep your energy levels high when training and always respond positively when your dog does what you want. If you start to flag and become unresponsive during training, the exercises will probably suffer.

4

Immediately after the dog has returned to you, throw the toy for a retrieve game.

5

When the dog brings the toy back, tell the dog how well it's done. Suddenly training becomes fun!

RECALL WITH A TOY

TRAINING WITH TWO TOYS

START: 1

Some dogs are reluctant to give up a toy that they have run to fetch. On such occasions it pays to have a second toy ready on hand that you can use as a substitute.

2

*Encourage the dog to run back to you with enthusiastic cries of **"Come."***

COMMAND
"COME"

Some dogs may not return with the toy. This is quite common, because they instinctively love possession. In this case bring out the second toy and use that one instead. The dog often leaves the first toy for the one you have in your hand. It's a general dog motto that if you have something, it must be better. Once the dog is coming each time you squeak the toy and command **"Come,"** we may add the Sit as a new link in the chain. Praise the dog and then say **"Free,"** which is the release command. Most dogs just keep looking at you in expectation as **"Free"** means nothing to them at first. Now ignore the dog and wander around the garden until it walks off to sniff something else. Now repeat the whole recall procedure again using the toy. Practice this between five and ten times a day throughout Week 1. If your dog is especially keen to come and is making fast progress, you may also practice on your walks in the park in the first week. Depending on your dog's enthusiasm, this training helps to embed the basis for the Recall in the park.

Problem Solving

The dog quickly loses interest in the toy
Solution:

- Change toys.
- Make sure your dog is getting no toys at other times.
- Are you training for too long a period?
- Are you training when the dog has low energy?
- Do you have two toys to use?

The dog stops coming halfway to you
Solution:

- As your dog slows down as it approaches, jump up and down animatedly and run backward.
- As your dog approaches you, lower your body and crouch a bit — it will be less intimidating for a lower ranking dog to approach you.
- Attach a short (2 m/6 ft.) light line to the dog's collar, so that you can take hold of it as the dog returns. It prevents the dog running off with the toy.

3

If the dog then refuses to give up the toy, show it the second toy that you are holding. Normally a dog will prefer something that its owner is holding and will drop the first toy.

4

Praise the dog and then repeat the procedure by throwing the second toy for a retrieve game. By switching the toy that you throw, you remain in control.

MAKING A GAME OF IT

START : 1

If your problem is a dog that starts off with the right intentions but stops when it is only halfway back to you, remember the importance of dramatics in training and act in a really animated way.

COMMAND
"COME"

COMMAND
"COME"

3

Praise the dog when it reaches you — it has to feel motivated and prepared to do the exercise again.

PRAISE
"GOOD DOG"

2

Command the dog to **"Come,"** jump up and down and run backward. Instantly the recall exercise has become a game again.

LEASH AND COLLAR RECALL

2

Turn away from the dog and walk out to the full length of the leash, taking care to allow a little slack so that it does not inadvertently pull on the dog's collar and disturb it from remaining in the sit position.

START : 1

For this method of teaching the recall you need to attach a 2 m (6 ft.) leash to your dog's collar. Command it to ***"Sit."***

COMMAND

"SIT"

Leash and Collar Recall

Commands **"Sit," "Stay"** and **"Come"** are used in conjunction with leash control.

Leash and collar recall is the basic system of training a dog to come. Place your dog on a leash and collar and then attach a 2 m (6 ft.) leash to the collar. Tell the dog to sit and stay, walk about 1 m (3 ft.) away, stop, about turn and after a few seconds call the dog's name to get its attention, and then firmly say **"Come."** Bend

down and when the dog approaches you, offer praise as it comes closer. After many successful practices, you can add the **"Sit"** command so that we have completed the entire recall.

Now many of you may already have achieved this, but find that working with the leash poses more problems. At least if your dog can achieve the above, it probably understands what you want before the next training techniques are used. Of course you should

Do not tug on the leash when you command **"Come."**

4
Give the dog some praise as it approaches you — these verbal encouragements help to motivate the animal and keep you as the focus of attention throughout the exercise.

3
Give the recall command in a firm tone of voice and bend toward the dog a little to encourage it to run to you.

COMMAND
"COME"

5
Reward the dog with plenty of strokes, pats and attention when it consistently comes on command. These rewards help to reinforce the Recall and make the dog happy to come to you when you ask it to.

also be teaching the sit, stand, down and stay positions daily, which helps with general obedience.

Practice this leash recall training in the home, in the yard and in the park. Once your dog is good at coming to you, add some distractions. For instance, get people to run past you or walk nearby with their dogs. If your dog reacts to the distraction and moves from its position, reinforce your commands in the way described on page 131.

SOUND AND FOOD RECALL

START : 1

The first step is to show your dog one of the food portions that you have prepared. Let the dog sniff it to find out what you have in your hand, but do not let it eat the food. That comes later...

2

*Run backward, command **"Come"** and then blow the whistle once.*

COMMAND
"COME"

Sound and Food Recall

With this exercise I recommend that your dog be eating a natural meat-based diet — I find results are much better if using a meat-based diet, as opposed to commercial dry foods with additives and colorants.

Dogs have good hearing and most dogs enjoy eating; this exercise draws on both these facts. You'll need a dog whistle and some food. Begin training in a quiet area of the park you have chosen or preferably in your own yard. Divide half the dog's normal daily food allowance into about ten portions and keep it in a container. For dogs that are very difficult to get back or are not that keen on food rewards, it pays to let the dog go hungry for a short while. Do not feed the dog for one whole day. Dogs can manage without food for

this period without harm, although this food reduction does not apply to pups under six months of age.

The next day begin your recall training in your yard. Show your dog a portion of food in your hand, let the dog sniff it and then run backward, simultaneously and excitedly commanding: "Rover, come!" and blow the whistle once. Your dog should follow the food and

Above: This recall method takes advantage of a dog's natural desire to eat. The daily food allowance should be divided into ten succulent portions which will be used as rewards when the dog obeys the recall command. Keep these in a container or pouch for easy access.

3

The incentive of a food reward should encourage the dog to come eagerly toward you.

4

When the dog arrives, praise it for being a "Good dog" and immediately let it have the food reward.

PRAISE

"GOOD DOG"

come to you. So reward it with a chunk as soon as it comes to you. At this stage the Sit is not important — we don't want to interrupt the dog's desire to come to you. Repeat this sequence ten times, and then stop the recall lesson — perhaps do some other training exercises. Any food you haven't used can be given to your dog during the next training session. The dog will have begun to link the word **"Come"** with the whistle sound and, upon arrival, a food treat that is not a tidbit but part of its daily diet. This is crucial.

Now your dog has a real incentive to come when called, for a dog's stomach usually rules its mind. You can use the remainder of its food for that day's second and third lessons. Continue the training for another three days until your dog comes when you command and whistle each time. Keep the dog on the hungry side during the first couple of weeks of training exercises, especially if it's not overtly food-focused. If your dog is, you may consider training in a quiet area of the park from Day 1. For most dogs, however, it is best to start in the yard until the dog begins to come reliably and without responding to distractions.

5

At this stage, there's no need to insist upon the Sit. That comes in the next phase which is described on page 137.

SOUND AND FOOD RECALL

Once your dog responds reliably, drop the verbal commands and use the whistle only, though you may continue to praise it as it runs toward you. Now begin to introduce the Sit. Once the dog is coming and sitting happily, attach the leash and practice the Heel for about three or four minutes. Then tell the dog to sit, praise it and then tell it to go **"Free"** and walk off. Then repeat the whole recall training with food again. This especially helps those dogs that have realized that the leash going on means home. The dog can never know when you are about to go home as you attach the leash many times during the walk.

This training requires perseverance, but it is worthwhile in the end to have a dog that comes when called. In the long run the dog will return to being fed at home through its food bowl, but in that case I take a little bag of ham or cheese chunks out with me and intermittently give the dog a treat for some of the recalls. It helps to maintain the training standards permanently.

Sound and Food Recall — Review

- Your dog learns that food now arrives at unspecified times during training either at home or outside.
- Your dog learns that the new whistle sound corresponds to food rewards.
- Your dog learns that obeying the command **"Sit"** ensures the delivery of more praise.
- Your dog no longer eats from a bowl at home for 21 days.

Training Tips

- Don't call your dog only to put its leash when it is time to go home.

- Call your dog at least ten times per walk to embed the Recall.

- Once the dog comes to you reliably, add the "Sit" command.

- Play a game of some sort with your dog during each walk to maintain its interest.

After 21 days and as your dog progresses with the Recall, you should use food rewards intermittently to reinforce the Recall. This means that the dog never knows if the food is going to be given but the chance that it may be offered occasionally maintains the Recall. Of course you will now have surplus food that can be given to the dog either on the last Recall or when you get home.

COMMAND
"COME"

TRAINING IN THE PARK

START : 1
The sound and food recall exercise is particularly useful for people who have mobility problems.

START : 1

As you progress with this recall method, just use the whistle to attract your dog's attention.

COMMAND
"SIT"

2

Now you can introduce **"Sit"** *at the conclusion of the exercise.*

3

Reward the dog's obedience with a succulent tidbit.

4

It pays dividends to finish off the exercise by attaching the leash and practicing some heelwork before letting your dog go free to play. It will no longer associate the leash just with the fact that it is time to go home.

2

The reward of a food tidbit is a powerful reason for obeying a recall command. The dog no longer expects its food only to be delivered through a food bowl.

3

You should always praise your dog when it comes and sits obediently on command.

LONG LINE RECALL

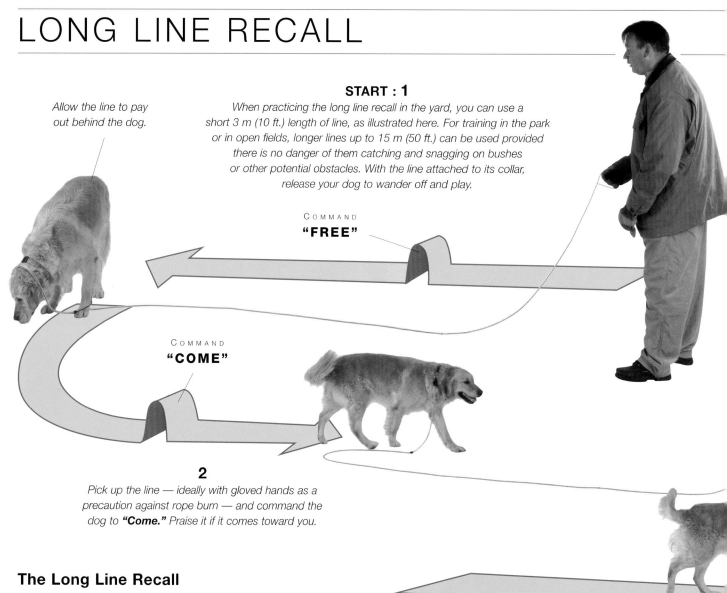

Allow the line to pay out behind the dog.

START : 1

When practicing the long line recall in the yard, you can use a short 3 m (10 ft.) length of line, as illustrated here. For training in the park or in open fields, longer lines up to 15 m (50 ft.) can be used provided there is no danger of them catching and snagging on bushes or other potential obstacles. With the line attached to its collar, release your dog to wander off and play.

COMMAND
"FREE"

COMMAND
"COME"

2

Pick up the line — ideally with gloved hands as a precaution against rope burn — and command the dog to "Come." Praise it if it comes toward you.

The Long Line Recall

Note: This method is intended for adult dogs or very large breed puppies only.

For this method you will need two lines, a pair of thick gardening gloves and food treats if they are being used. (These treats are not the dog's main diet, as in the Sound and Food Reward described above.) Until the advent of spray collars (see page 39), the long line was the only method that enabled you to compel your dog to do your wishes at a distance, though the skill to master the line takes a week or so to achieve. You will need a 10–15 m (33–50 ft.) piece of line, for instance the unbreakable nylon cord sold in most hardware stores. A dog hook is attached to one end of the line

and a loop like that on the leash is made at the other end. I tend to wrap the line around a thick stick to prevent it from getting tangled. When using the long line in the park, avoid trees, bushes, park benches or other objects that the line may get looped around. Open fields and parks are best. I also have a shorter 3 m (10 ft.) line on hand for when training in my backyard. Again, check your yard for obvious items the line may get tangled on when the dog is running free.

Yard Recall

Release your dog in the yard on the line with the command **"Free."** Now ignore the dog until it walks off for a sniff. Put your gloves on and now take the line in your hand (the glove stops rope burn if the dog pulls away suddenly). You can pick the line up at any point — not just at its end — and take up the slack without pulling. Call your dog, **"Rover! Come."** If he comes, praise him as he comes and then release him again. If he bounces around you, always drop the line completely so as not to get it tangled. Say **"Free"** again. When he bounds off, repeat the exercise several more times. If you want, give him a treat when he comes obediently to help reinforce the idea.

3

If your dog turns and comes toward you in response to the recall command, praise it in an animated tone of voice and start to gather up the line loosely to keep it out of the way of your dog's legs.

4

This dog is coming obediently on command. Take care not to pull on the line — it must be loose.

5

When a dog responds correctly to a recall, the long line is simply an adjunct to the training that is not called into play. However, if a dog should ignore you, then the line can be used to gain the dog's attention — this technique is explained on the next page.

6

Once the exercise is completed successfully, release your dog and repeat it a few more times.

LONG LINE RECALL

THE SNAP CHECK

START : 1

The long line proves its usefulness when you are dealing with a dog that persistently ignores the command to "Come."

The golden retriever is not paying attention.

COMMAND
"COME"

COMMAND
"COME"

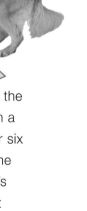

If your dog ignores you, which many do, or continues its own business of exploring, repeat the command **"Come"** and simultaneously snap the line sharply, using both your hands if dealing with a large dog. (Puppies and or delicate breeds under six months should receive a slight tug only.) Nylon line "gives" so by the time the snap reaches the dog's collar, it is experienced as a mild tug. This irritant generally gets the dog to at least look at you. Some dogs become unsure at this action and they begin to listen. (Never attempt to haul or drag the dog in.) As the dog takes notice, call **"Come"** again if it has not already started to run toward you. As the dog comes, praise it enthusiastically — for less motivated dogs a little dramatics will help here — jump up and down and run backward as the dog arrives or is heading toward you. This excites the dog, improves its confidence and keeps its attention.

When the dog arrives, a pat and maybe a tidbit will help to reinforce the new ideas. Now take hold of the line about 20 cm (8 in.) from the dog's collar and let the rest of the line fall to the ground. You now can use the line like a normal leash. Tell the dog to **"Sit"** and finish with praise.

Practice this many more times until your dog responds each and every time without having to be snapped by the line, and comes willingly for the reward and fun of being with you. You will now be in a position to praise your dog for coming, rather than chasing it about the yard in frustration repeating endless commands.

COMMAND
"COME"

At the end of the exercise, some words of praise, pats and strokes and perhaps a tidbit will all serve as powerful rewards that your dog will associate with the action of running to you when called.

2

If the dog does not respond, give a sharp snap on the line to gain its attention once more. Remember — it's just a snap; do not physically drag the dog toward you.

3

Start to gather in the line as the dog comes back to you.

4

*Command **"Come"** again and encourage the dog to run all the way back to you with enthusiastic praise and animated body language.*

NAP THE
LINE

COMMAND
"COME"

START : 1

If your dog seems listless or lacking in motivation while training, try to make your "performance" eye-catching.

COMMAND
"COME"

ACTION AND REACTION

2

Wave your arms and run backward — it's worth trying any tactic that will encourage the dog to run toward you.

TRAINING IN THE PARK

Training in the Park

As soon as your dog will come to you reliably, you are ready to try this training method in the park using a long line up to 200 m (600 ft.) in length. Some of you will feel confident enough to skip the yard training because you live in areas where there are few distractions in public places. This is fine.

It is important to mention here a little bit about the psychology of line use. When a dog is released in the park, it often runs a good distance away from you, and certainly more than the 15 m (45 ft.) of line. That's fine. Don't hold the line like a flexi-leash — it's not a long leash. If the dog constantly finds that it reaches the end of the line and then experiences a stop, it learns the limits of your control and the length of the line. I never want a dog to learn this. If possible try to call the dog back before it reaches the line's end. You can pick up the line at any point, not just the end. Just before the line is about to become taut tell the dog to **"Come."** If it turns and does so, mission accomplished! Finish the exercise as above. Make the dog sit, wait a few seconds and then release it again. Practice this as many times as possible.

If the dog runs about 100 m (300 ft.) away, the line will be fully let out trailing behind it. Casually walk toward the dog and pick the line up. Wrap it around your gloved hand and call the dog again. If it responds — good. If it is slow to respond or carries on doing its own thing, then snap the line sharply to remind it that you are there and it should come.

The fact that the dog can be up to 200 m (600 ft.) away from you with the line trailing behind never seems to help the dog to understand how long the line is. It simply remembers that if it does not respond

LONG-LINE TRAINING

While the dog is allowed to run free in the park at some distance from you, let the line trail along behind it. Don't keep hold of it or the dog will experience a series of snaps at inappropriate times.

START : 1   **2**

when you call there is an interruption to what it is doing, and a great reward when it responds.

Some dogs run halfway toward you and then stop or hesitate. I always run backward repeating the **"Come"** command and praising the dog only when it moves in my direction. This tends to encourage the dog to come to you.

Dealing with Problems

If your dog does happen to snag the line on anything, simply clip its normal leash onto its collar for control, and unclip the long line while you sort out the snag.

Though many dogs learn to come quite quickly on the line, I keep using it for longer than 21 days, and test the dog in as many locations as possible to help reinforce the training. Sometimes I will use a squeaky toy, ball or other inducement to help speed the dog's wish to come to me on command. Remember: if it helps, use it.

The next question is when to stop using the line and how to go about discontinuing it. If you simply take the line off, many dogs revert to being disobedient. Once you no longer need to snap the dog down the line — in other words when your dog comes on command all the time — then shorten the line by one-

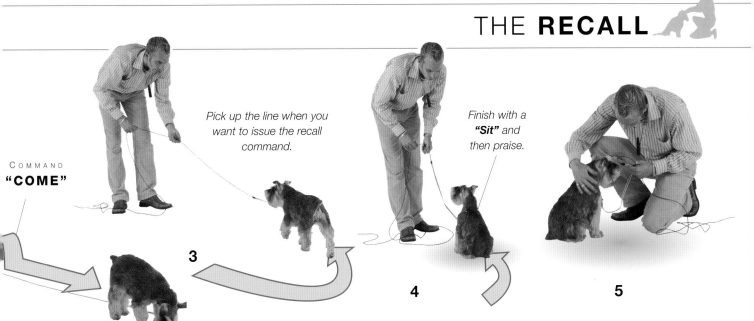

COMMAND
"COME"

Pick up the line when you want to issue the recall command.

3

Finish with a **"Sit"** *and then praise.*

4

5

*Above: This sequence (**1-5**) shows how a long line can be used as part of recall training. Here the dog comes obediently when called and falls into the Sit when the owner so instructs him. If, however, he should ignore the command to* **"Come,"** *the line can be sharply snapped to refocus the dog's attention on what he should be doing.*

quarter of its length each week. Finish by leaving just 1 m (3 ft.) of line on the dog for a few more weeks to serve as a little psychological reminder. The line weight should not disappear in one day.

Long Line Recall — Review
- Your dog learns that when it ignores you, a snap will come down the line.
- When your dog runs to you, act pleased and interested.
- When your dog arrives, lavish more praise, then command **"Sit,"** more praise and maybe run backward.
- A treat may also be a pleasant reward for coming.

Problem Solving
Other dogs try to play with a dog and get tangled in the line
Solution:
Only use the line in places with few other dogs around

until the Recall has been mastered. If a dog does interrupt you, call your dog in, detach the line and connect its leash. Leave the line on the ground and quickly walk off with your dog on the leash. You can return for the line a few minutes later.

The line gets tangled around the dog's legs
Solution:
Most dogs step out of the tangle of their own accord, but as soon as their owners intercede, the dog turns around excitedly and gets further tangled. The easiest way out of a tangle is to disconnect the line and allow it to fall on the ground. The dog can then step out.

The dog returns but immediately runs off again
Solution:
Step on the line so you can stop the dog running off, then take hold of it and use it as a leash. As the dog returns, connect its leash to prevent the problem. As the dog approaches you, command **"Sit"** just as it gets near, then take hold of its collar.

If the dog runs past you on its return, command **"Sit"** when it is at least 2 m (6 ft.) away from you. This slows it down.

Always praise your dog for each separate action.

FLEXI-LEASHES AND WHISTLES

Using Flexi-Leashes (puppy safe)

A flexible or flexi-leash is a long line and hook that is spring-loaded, allowing it to rewind automatically into a plastic reel with a handle. These can be used like a leash for teaching the recall exercise over varying distances. However, they cannot be used instead of the long line for teaching recall as the dog would have to drag the large plastic handle unit behind it, which is impractical and defeats the psychology of line training. Flexi-leashes are often used for young puppies and for food recall training, where they are helpful for gaining initial control.

Whistle Recall

Using a whistle can really help when training a dog to come. Of course the dog generally knows what **"Come"** means but doesn't necessarily realize that it should respond immediately rather than coming when it wants. By using the whistle it receives a clear signal over a far greater distance and will come to recognize a consistent sound. You can use the whistle with a gamut of different training methods. It can be combined with food, toys, praise or even a game of hide and seek.

Begin in the house or yard. Make sure your dog has not eaten that day, or better still for more reluctant dogs, use its food as the training tidbits. Use solid chunks of meat. Dry food is neither recommended nor useful.

The structure of this exercise is similar to that using a toy except that the stimulus to respect the command **"Come"** is now the food. Always begin whistle recall training in the house and then progress to the yard. It takes most dogs only half a dozen recalls to get the message.

START : 1
Here a whistle is used to attract the puppy's attention in readiness for the "Come" command.

2
As the puppy approaches, the flexi-leash rewinds into its plastic handle.

WHISTLE TEST — TRAINING AT LONG DISTANCE

The beauty of using a whistle is that the sound will carry clearly over a greater distance than a voice command is likely to do. This can be vital for owners who are not always able to keep up with an energetic dog in the park.

START : 1
The dog is coming in response to the whistle signal.

USING A FLEXI-LEASH

3

When the puppy reaches you in response to the whistle signal, encourage it to sit still at your feet.

C O M M A N D
"SIT"

5

Note how the long flexi-leash has rewound entirely onto its reel. The trainer can use both hands to stroke and reward the obedient pup.

4

*Once the puppy has obeyed the **"Sit"** command, you can give it a little food tidbit.*

Once again the dog is commanded to sit and then is rewarded with verbal praise, pats and a food tidbit for an exemplary performance.

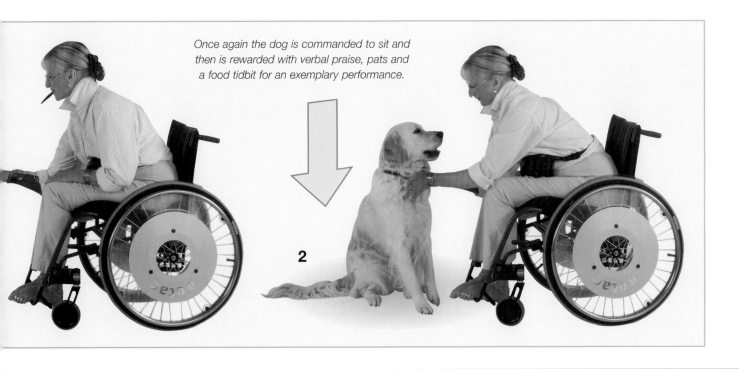

2

WHISTLE RECALL

When your dog is paying little attention and is a short distance from you, call its name, command **"Come"** and blow the whistle once. If the dog makes little connection, approach it with the food treat near its nose and let it follow the food toward you as you walk backward a few steps.

The critical point is that the dog should follow you. As it does so, repeat the command **"Come"** and blow the whistle again, but omit its name. Immediately give the food reward. Ignore the dog again until it walks off. Most dogs actually respond quickly, though puppies often need to use their noses to follow the food in your hand due to their undeveloped sense of coordination.

Once your dog gets the idea that the sound of the whistle brings a food reward upon arrival at your feet, you can drop the verbal command **"Come"** and just use the whistle followed by a treat on arrival. The train-ing will now speed up. If your dog responds very well, sometimes it is difficult to get the dog to leave you alone. This actually means that we have to play Ignore for longer, so you can use the whistle time and time again.

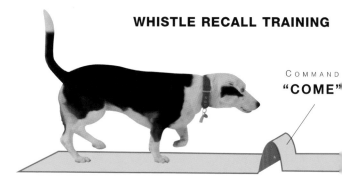

START : 1
*Whistle recall training combines the sound of a whistle, the command **"Come"** and a food reward that is used to encourage a dog to obey its trainer.*

WHISTLE RECALL TRAINING

COMMAND
"COME"

SLEEPERS AWAKE!
While in the house, if a dog is lying in the front room or near the front door asleep, I will blow the whistle so the dog can hear the sound even though it is out of your sight. **When it arrives, you truly know that the dog has learned the sound and food reward.** Again this will be useful when the dog is out of sight in the home or park.

Well-trained dogs respond to the whistle even when they are sleeping or out of your sight.

Keeping Puppies on Track

It is quite possible to teach the Recall to a puppy but you should remember that because of its young age, its attention span will be relatively brief and it is liable to get distracted during training. Physically a puppy also lacks the high levels of coordination that an adult dog enjoys, and so you may need to hold the food in your hand quite close to a puppy's nose to allow it to "follow the scent" all the way to you.

2
*While the dog is sniffing around oblivious to you, call its name, command **"Come"** and blow the whistle clearly.*

3
By running backward with the tidbit held out enticingly as a treat, you make the dog follow you. You can blow the whistle again to reinforce the desired signal.

4
Make sure that you give the tidbit as a reward as soon as the dog is sitting obediently at your feet.

5
Eventually the dog should respond to the whistle alone. You now have a useful new tool in your training kit.

Above: This dachshund puppy has its eyes firmly on the tidbit that its owner is holding just in front of its nose. You can use this keen response to food to start to teach a puppy the Recall.

HIDE AND SEEK

Hide and Seek Recall

If a dog is a pack animal, why on earth do we have such trouble getting them back at times? Well, of course, being part of a pack doesn't mean that the dogs cling together like glue. A wolf pack can operate in a loose fashion and so a dog a kilometer (2.5 mi.) or more away from you still considers itself within the pack. The bottom line is that like wolves, dogs generally hunt as a pack, but can also hunt alone.

This training method takes advantage of the fact that dogs are pack animals that find it natural to move, hunt and roam together. The relationship you have with your dog needs to be close in order to take advantage of these natural tendencies. If you use this method, you need to have already built a relationship with the dog where you are deferred to as the leader (see the Leadership Program in Chapter 3).

Pick a safe place where there are few roads so that if your dog does lose you momentarily, it won't get

hurt. When your dog is about 50 m (150 ft.) away from you, hide behind a tree or bush. Most dogs will want to keep you in sight even if they do not reliably obey your commands until taught otherwise. While hiding, call the dog's name and command **"Come."** After a short time the dog will notice your disappearance. If your dog comes running to seek you out, it will begin to panic a little when you do not appear. Let this happen, then show yourself. As your dog runs up to

you repeat the command **"Come"** and indulge in a bit of dramatic praise, running and jumping as if this is the most exciting event in your life. Maybe throw a toy for the dog also.

Now repeat this many times as you walk each day. The dogs this method works with become harder and harder to hide from. My dog that is well trained still loves this game of hide and seek and it keeps him on his toes. Thereafter you can use the command **"Come"** and the dog will be determined to arrive immediately before you can do the disappearing trick. Sometimes a tidbit helps to reinforce the message.

When the dog hears your call or whistle but is unable to spot you hiding in the trees, it should start to seek you out.

Once you have got the hang of hide and seek recall, you can repeat the training method from time to time while you are out walking with your dog. It will be eager to come and find you before you go "missing" again.

Above: When your dog successfully finds you, reinforce the sense of reassurance it will feel with lots of praise and strokes.

HIDE AND SEEK RECALL

This is an effective recall method to use with dogs that like to wander off from you while you are out walking. Although your dog may seem to be unconcerned about your whereabouts, it does like to be reassured that the pack leader is in the vicinity. By hiding from your dog, and calling or whistling it to **"Come"** while you are hidden, you arouse a slight sense of confusion and anxiety. The dog will be eager to run up to you when you do reappear and issue the **"Come"** command again.

While the dog is hunting left and right in an attempt to find you, pop out into view again and call **"Come."**

USING A SPRAY COLLAR

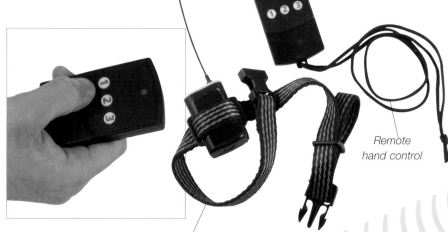

Aerial and spray unit

Remote hand control

Remote Spray Collars

These are the latest devices to help people control their dog's behavior at a distance. They contain an innocuous spray, like citronella or mustard scent. When the handset is depressed a jet of citronella spray is released from the collar beneath the dog's chin forming a cloud of vapor under the dog's nose. The psychological effect on the dog is similar to (but stronger than) a snap sent down the long line, and causes the following:

- It is alarming and the dog is happy to run back to the owner calling them.
- The dog's determined sniffing or play is suddenly interrupted, allowing it to hear the **"Come"** command once more.

It is important that you are skilled in dog training before using a collar. In my experience they should only be sold to people who are prepared to pay for a qualified dog trainer to work with them and who can explain the correct use of the collar. The instructions packaged with the collar often take no account of an individual's knowledge and many people end up wasting their money. Ask a trainer for assistance.

SPRAY COLLAR RECALL

A spray collar works by startling a dog that is ignoring your commands. It delivers an unpleasant sensory experience — in this case a shrill sound and pungent smell — that the dog finds unrewarding. It discovers that there is more enjoyment to be had in obeying the recall command than in ignoring you as it had previously done.

The remote hand control unit activates the collar.

START : 1

The jet of strong-smelling vapor emitted by the collar interrupts a dog's meanderings. The dog will probably look up in a startled way.

C O M M A N D
"COME"

2

While the dog is feeling a little alarmed and looking around for you, command **"Come"** again.

3

The dog should come running back for reassurance. Praise it as it approaches and let it know that it's been a **"Good dog."** But one word of warning — ask for professional advice before using a spray collar for the first time.

P R A I S E
"GOOD DOG"

Recall Dos and Don'ts

Don'ts

• Don't chase a dog that does not come on command. It simply makes a game of it and inhibits the training process.

• Don't shout at your dog. It causes the dog to associate recall with your anger — not what you want at all.

• Don't catch your dog and then hit it for not coming to you sooner. Dogs don't make that sort of connection.

• Don't train in areas that make your task more difficult with regard to outside distractions. Add these slowly over a period of several weeks.

• Don't train after a walk — dogs lose interest or fail to obey because they are worn out.

• Don't call your dog if you are unable to reinforce the command if you are ignored, even if that means that the dog goes where you may not wish it to. That way your dog learns that when you speak, it has no choice but to obey.

Dos

• Do ensure you know what you are about to do.

• Do make sure you have all your equipment and that any treats or tidbits are readily available.

• Do change your location or do some other leash training if the dog appears difficult.

• Do make sure you can train your dog with several different exercises and finish on one it can do well.

CHAPTER ELEVEN

Keeping It Going

Once your dog is trained according to the 21-day program, it should be relatively easy for you to maintain and even improve the standard of obedience you have reached. As mentioned previously, factors like age, breed and your personal circumstances will ultimately dictate your progress and the end result.

Completing the section on location training (pages 110–11) will help you to embed the training in all the places that are part of your lifestyle. If you live in the city, the concentration of dogs, people and crosswalks encountered there will require a greater need for obedience and good heeling from your dog while negotiating a busy street. Rural dog owners will need to be more aware of farms and wild animals, and so recall will be more pertinent to them. Heel training will be less important because of the wide spaces available to the dog.

Try to practice some training exercises every time you go out with your dogs. I do, and it certainly pays dividends in terms of their obedience.

Combining Training with a Walk

When I am out walking my dogs, passing dog owners often comment "Oh aren't your dogs well behaved" or "I wish my dog was so obedient." It's as if the person thinks that my dogs are naturally easy to manage. Of course this person probably spends the same time walking their dog as I do, but I train and practice as I go — they simply walk and, more often than not, put up with their dog's antics. My dogs are well trained because I make an effort and reinforce my dogs' view that I am the leader.

I practice training my own dogs virtually every time I go into town or for a walk in the local hills. My dogs, Saffie (a cairn terrier) and Gist (a German shepherd), are told to lie down and stay while I open the back of the Jeep in the driveway of my house. No mad dash to get in is allowed. They enter the vehicle on my command of **"In."**

When we arrive at the place where we're going to enjoy a country walk, the dogs are told to stay in the back of the Jeep while I open the door. That's the "Down/Stay" position. I open the door, wait about ten seconds and then call the dogs out and to me. That involves the Recall and Sit in front of me. Again, I tell the dogs to stay and wait a short time then say **"Free."** Off they go for their 8 km (5 mi.) walk off the leash. That repetition helps reinforce the training and keeps my dogs listening to me — the leader of the pack.

On the walk I will sometimes call my dogs to me if I see another dog in the distance walking toward me, especially if it's a small dog. Some small dog owners become anxious when a large German shepherd runs toward their pet. By calling my dogs to me and then putting them in the heel position, it demonstrates to the other dog walker that my dogs are under control. If all is well, I release my dogs on command and the dogs all say hello, and play together. My dogs learn to focus on me when other dogs appear rather than dashing off because they are attracted by the other dog. This subtle practice in training reinforces the lessons that an obedience-trained dog must learn. Whatever the circumstances, my dogs are taught that they must always listen and obey.

Even if I meet no other dogs on my walk, I will still call Gist and Saffie to me several times and tell them to sit upon arrival. I pause and tell them they are "good dogs" and release them once more. Near the end of the walk, about 200 m (600 ft.) before I reach my Jeep, I call both my dogs to heel and we walk under control to my vehicle. This is another example of how dogs learn: my dogs now automatically — without a command — come to heel of their own volition when I am about 200 m (600 ft.) from my jeep. I always praise them and now the routine is well established. That shows clearly how dogs learn and how you can practice your training daily out in the real world — hopefully for your dog's entire life.

Should I Join a Training Club?

Many dog owners train their dogs by joining a local dog training club. Unfortunately some end up disillusioned by what they are taught and may stop attending the club either out of boredom at the way the lessons are staged, or because the club just does not have instructors who inspire them. To avoid this situation, it's a good idea to visit training clubs before joining, so that you can watch what goes on and how things are organized. Among the many thousands of dog training clubs and professional trainers in operation, there are many that are superb. But take the time to find one that inspires you. Even once you have trained your dog using this book, it makes sense to test your dog's obedience in the company of other dog enthusiasts under expert guidance at such venues. The idea of dog training is to teach your dog practical skills, so you should always take the chance of reinforcing these skills when the opportunity arises.

CHAPTER TWELVE

Troubleshooting

As a professional dog trainer, I have to deal with an enormous variety of temperaments and breeds (both canine and human) when I begin to train a group of dogs. As well as sizing up the individual dogs, I need to assess how good the owners are at learning and then putting lessons into practice. When problems occur in training I always tell my students to look at themselves before criticizing their dog's progress — the owner is the conduit of knowledge, not the dog.

Unless you are very fortunate, it's almost inevitable that you will hit some problems in the course of the training program. This chapter looks at what may be going wrong and gives some tips for getting things back on track.

Perhaps your dog is very good at most of the exercises, but is still quite resistant to the Recall. That exercise, then, needs reviewing. Look at the methods you have been employing, and perhaps select a new one from the options that I have given you in this book. I find that the most likely cause of resistance to an exercise is previously embedded bad behavior. Most dogs will train for the Recall well, but if your dog is struggling then break down the component part of the exercise at which the dog is failing. Perhaps the reward of food is not a strong enough motivator for your particular dog. If so, cut down the dog's overall food intake for a week or so, and only feed the dog on the walk during which you practice the Recall. Alternatively use a favorite toy as a motivator instead of food.

If your dog cannot resist distractions — in other words if it refuses to listen to you in training — don't continue to bang your head against the wall. This simply teaches your dog that you are ineffective as a leader. Seek out a quieter training area and work there until the dog is responding consistently well. Then move back to the previous training place. You need to be pragmatic. When problems arise, always place yourself in a position where you have maximum control over the surroundings. For positive training success, circumstances must be in your favor, not the dog's.

A Helping Hand

If you have a large dog like a Dalmatian and find that during the early stages of training it tires you out or appears to be getting the upper hand, then ask a friend to share the training with you — split the walk into sections so that the dog has two trainers. Have a break and think about the next exercise, while your friend practices some of the training routines. Moreover, a friend can often spot your handling errors if they are apparent, and help to boost your confidence and share in the fun of watching your dog improve.

Make sure your equipment is always on hand. If you are using a long line for the Recall and forget the line one day, don't release the dog. If you do, it will quickly notice that the line weight is missing and that you cannot snap it if it ignores your command **"Come."** Your previous good work will be undone and it will be harder for you to assert control.

Often, other dog owners decide to give you the benefit of their "wisdom" and will chip in with comments like "Oh just let him enjoy himself and run around." Smile, ignore them and continue with your training. That sort of wisdom is no help. Most dogs can do as they please for almost the entire day, so concentrating on training for a few minutes is no hardship. What's more, the dog will receive its fun and games after your lesson has been completed. Remember, training is designed to be fun. It means the dog has your undivided attention, it receives lots of praise for obeying your commands, plays ball retrieve games and much more. It is enjoying the privilege of you, the leader, interacting socially with it. Once the main training is complete, the dog's time is its own and it will be free to enjoy itself, but you can rest secure knowing that when you need to call your dog it will respond and want to come to you.

If you have friends who also own dogs and are interested in training together, then after Week 1 of the program why not arrange to meet? The more dogs the merrier and the controlled distractions created by the proximity of other dogs will again help to teach your dog to listen to you in such circumstances.

What If I Own Two Dogs?

Many people own two or more dogs. The training information in this book will apply to all the dogs if required. However, I find that when most people present problem dogs to me and say that they own two dogs, generally just one of the dogs needs to be improved though training. This can be the case when the second dog is from a rescue center. Such animals often have training and behavioral problems.

Sometimes clients who have a really well-behaved dog get a puppy and this turns into a really difficult dog to train. They cannot understand why, because their first dog is so obedient and they use the same training methods. This can be for numerous reasons, often connected with the way dogs learn and how they relate to each other in packs. Two children often turn out very differently even though they are reared in the same family. However, normally people who have trained and managed one dog well tend to manage the second just as competently.

If you have one dog that is proving more difficult to train than another, then place it on the training plan in this book and only take that dog out for training. Don't bring the second dog along as a distraction until the untrained dog has been properly trained. It's a common fault that an owner will try to train a dog while simultaneously attempting to handle a second. The commands are picked up by both dogs, even if the commands are preceded by individual names. This is confusing and prevents effective and consistent training. Once the untrained dog is obeying you and performing to a high standard, begin to introduce the other dog on the walks. Even then you must insist on the newly trained dog performing its obedience tasks while the well-behaved dog is running free, just to let it know that you command it in all situations. In time, you will have two happy trained dogs enjoying life in your company.

Also, as previously recommended, consider having a second person help in these situations. This will allow you to concentrate on the problem dog and let you develop new training skills. Over time both dogs should happily adapt and obey you when out together.

Index

Note: Page numbers set in *italic type* refer to picture captions; page numbers set in **bold type** refer to a photo sequence showing an exercise in progress.

A

acknowledgment of good behavior *47*, 49

aggression 14-15, *14*, 38

    toward dogs 14, *125*

    toward people 14

anxieties 15

attention

    attracting dog's by owner 34, *63*, *72*, *74*, *86*, *115*, *119*, *124*, *125*, 128, 132, *133*, *139*

    giving by owner 21, *21*, 26, 27, 46

    paying by dog 68, *68*, *69*, 71, *72*

    seeking by dog 13, 20, 21, 26, *26*, 29, 49

    withholding by owner *see* Ignore, the

B

barking 8, 29, 42, 49

bedrooms, access to 22, 27

beds, dog 22, 40-1, *41*

boisterous behavior 21, 28, 42, 90, 109

boxers 21

breed-specific behavior 10, 18, 45, 49, 59

C

car harness 36

cars

    entering 54, 79, 152

    getting out of 12, 54, 78, 79, **78-9**

    heelwork as element of car training 76-9, **76-7**

cats 37

chairs, access to 23, *23*

chase behavior, predatory 15, 16

chasing 18, 58, 112, 124

    livestock 39

chewing 31, 32, 40, *41*, *42*, 47

children and dogs *18*, 19, *19*, 46

citronella 39, 150

classes, puppy socialization 34

clubs, training 14, 153

collar and leash

    control with 24, 28, 29, 34, *46*, 47, *47*, 62, 80, 84, *92*, 93, 94, 95, 102, **102-3**, 105, 108, **108**, 110, *122*, *132-3*, **132-3**

    introduction of 33, *33*, 62-3

collars 38-9

    chain 35, 36, 39

    choosing 36

    face 36, 38-9, *38*, 80-1, *80*, *81*, 82

    half-slip 36

    head *see* face

    high check *see* slip

    remote training 39, *39; see also* collars, spray

    slip 35, 39, 82-3, *83*

    spray 138, 150-1, **150-1**; *see also* collars, spray; deterrents, sprays

collies 18

"Come" command 12, 17, 32, 54, **56**, 78, *79*, *86*, 88, *92*, *101*, *113*, *127*, 128, *128*, 130, *131*, 132, *133*, 134, *134*, 135, *138*, 139, 140, *140*, *141*, 142, *143*, 144, *144*, 146, *146*, *147*, 148, *148*, 150, *151*, 154; *see also* recall exercises

communication 20, 27, 44-51, 59, 60, 64

compulsion training 9, 10

consistency in training 48, 49

D

deferential behavior 20, 48, 92, *100*

demotion *23*

deterrents

    sound 42

    sprays 40, *41; see also* citronella

    taste 47

diet 42, 43, 134

    natural 43

discs, training 31, 42, *42*

distractions 58, 86, 110-1, *110*, 112, *115*, *116*, 118, 122, *122*, *123*, 133, 135, 142, 151, 154, 155

dominant behavior 13, 20, 21, 23, *23*, *25*, 27, 28, 29, 31, 88 doorbells 8, 28

doors, going through 20, 21, 24, 113, **112-3**

down exercises 32, 35, 45, 50, 54, 55, **56**, 84, *85*, 106-11, 114

down/stay 35, 41, *41*, 55, 106, 110, 114, 118, 120, 122, 152

hand signal **50**

using a collar and leash 108, **108**

using a hook 109, **109**

using a push 110, **111**

using a toy 106, **106-7**

using food 106, **107**

E

equipment 36-43

F

fear 12, 48

feeding 24-5

"Fetch" command **16**, 54; *see also* retrieve

flexi-leashes 34, 35, 36, 37, *37*, 56, 144, **144-5**

food; *see also* tidbits, treats

as training aid 10, 32, 33, 34, 35, 38, 42-3, *43*, 46, 56, *63*, 68, *68*, 72, 84, *85*, 86, *86*, *87*, 90, *91*, 93, 94, 101, 104, 106, *107*, 108, 109, 116, 134-7, **134-5**, **136-7**, 138, 144, *145*, 146, *146*, 147, *147*, 151, 154

begging for 25

stealing 42

food toys 28, *28*, 29, 40

"Free" command 55, **56**, 78, 130, 136, 139, 153

furniture, keeping off 23, 27; *see also* chairs, access to

G

games 23, 26, *32*, 35, 55, 56, 59, 62, *63*, 121, *121*, 123, 127, 136, 154

hide and seek 144

retrieve *16*, *17*, *105*, 127, *127*, *129*, *131*, 155

gates, childproof 22

German shepherds 43

guarding behavior 8

guilt 48, 49

H

hand signals *48*, 50-1, 88, *89*, *92*, 94-5, **94-5**, *96*, 116, 117, *118*, *119*

harnesses

body 36

head *see* collars, face

walking (anti-pulling) 36-7, *37*, 82, *82*, **82-3**

heelwork exercises **17**, *33*, 35, 37, 38, *41*, 54, 55, **56**, 58, 60-83, **61**, **64-5**, 114, *114*, *115*, 136, 152, 153

and turns 64

car training 76-9, **76-7**

figure-eight pattern 72, **72-3**

for puppies 62-3, **63**

garden training 72-3

indoor training 71, **71**

lagging behind 70, **70**, *113*

left about turn 67, **66-7**, 75

left turns 66, **66-7**, *71*, 73

practice 70-1

right about turn 68, **68-9**, 75

right turns 68, **68-9**, *71*, 72, *72*

street 74-5

walking forward 64-5

herding behavior 17

hierarchy 20, 44; *see also* rank

hook restriction program 23, 28-9, 35, 41

hooks, wall 12, 23, 28, *28*, 29, 40, 90, *90*, *91*, 104, *104*, 109, **109**, 120, *120*

hounds 45

hunting instinct **16**

I

Ignore, the 26-7, *26*, 29, 49, 146

and sit 88, **88-9**

introduction to other pets 37

J-K

jumping up 13, 28, 34, 42

in puppies *32*

L

Labradors 21, 43, 70

landings, access to 22

Leadership Program 18, 20-9, *21*, 31, 40, 54, 59, 71, 113, 114, 148
  duration of 27
leashes 36; *see also* collar and leash
  snap-checking with *46*, 47, *47*, 58, 64, *64*, *65*, 68, 70, 72, 74, 140, *140*, *141*, 142, *143*
  flexible *see* flexi-leashes
  indoor training 71
lines, long 34, 36, 37, 56, 138-143, **138-9**, **140-1**, **142-3;** *see also* flexi-leashes
  tangles in 143
living rooms, access to 23, 27
locations, training 58, 70, *81*, 86, 96, 98, 110-1, *110*, 112, 118, 142, 151, 152

M

motivation 10, 14, 25, *25*, 32, *33*, 35, 48, 50, 59, 62, 126, *129*, *131*, 140, *141*, 154
mouthing 31, 40, *41*
  deterrents against *41*
moving out of the way 24, **24-5**

N

"No" command 42, 46, 47, 54, 60, 118
nudging 13, 49

O

overattachment 12

P-Q

pack behavior 11, 13, 20, 21, 26, 30, 44, *45*, 46, 49, 148

patting *21*, 23, 49, 140, *141*
Pekingese 45
phobias 15
  noise 43
picking up, demanding 21
play 8, 32, 46, 58, 70, *89*, 114, 124, *124*, 126, *137*
play-biting 40
playpens 32
praise 10, 21, 28, 45, 49, 54, 56, 59, 60, *61*, *63*, 64, *67*, 68, *69*, 71, *72*, 74, 75, *79*, 86, *87*, 88, *89*, *90*, *91*, 92, *92*, *93*, 94, 95, *95*, 96, *97*, 101, *101*, 106, *107*, 109, *109*, 110, *111*, 113, *114*, *115*, 116, 117, *117*, 118, *119*, 120, *120*, *127*, 128, *128*, *129*, *131*, *133*, *135*, 136, *137*, 140, *141*, 142, 143, 144, *145*, 148, *149*, *151*
pulling 12-13, 36-7, 38, *38*, 60, *61*, 64, *65*, 74, 75, *75*, 76, 80, 82, *82*, *83*, 84, *113*, 114; *see also* heelwork exercises
punishment 46, 47, 49, 124
puppies 10, 14, *15*, 18, 30-5, *30*, *31*, *32*, 40, 47, *125*, *126*, 140, 146, 155
  concentration span of 31, 34, *34*
  critical period for 45, 49, 125, 126
  one or two 30, *30*
puppy training 30-5, *32*, *33*, 54, 55, 83, 84, *85*, 86, *87*, 125, 126-7, **127**, 137, 138, 144, *144-5*, 147, *147*
  heelwork with 62-3, **63**
  plan 35

R

rank 24, 27, 47, 100, *100*, 104; *see also* hierarchy
recall exercises 10, 15, 17, 32, 37, 39, 40, 42, 54, 55, **56**, 58, 59, 84, 114, 124-151, 152, 153, 154; *see also* "Come" command
  dos and don'ts 151
  garden 139, 142, 144
  hand signal **50**
  hide and seek 148-9, **148-9**
  leash and collar 132-3, **132-3**
  long line 138-143, **138-9**, **140-1**
  park, in the 142-3
  problems, reasons for 124-5, *124*, *125*
  puppy training 32, 35, 125, 126-7, **127**
  using a spray collar 150-1, **150-1**
  using a toy 128-131, **128-9**, **130-1**
  using sound and food 134-7, **134-5**, **136-7**
  whistle 144-7, **144-5**, **146-7**
reinforcement, positive 9, 58
release command 54, **56**, 78, 130
remote-training collar *see* collars, remote-training
rescue dogs 59, 84, 90, 155
retrieve 54, 55, *103*, 126, 127, 128, *129*, *131*; *see also* games
reward-only-based training 9
rewards 10, 11, 16, 21, 23, *27*, 28, 29, 32, *33*, 41, 42, *43*, 44, 46, 48, 49, 56, 59, 60, *63*, 67, 72, *72*, 79, 80, *81*, 84, 86, *87*, *89*, 90, *93*, 99, 101, *101*, 102, *103*, 104, 113, 116, 128, 135, *135*, *137*, 140,

141, 142, *145*, 154; *see also*
food, praise, tidbits, treats, toys as
training aids

S

Saint Bernard 45

scavenging 39

scruff, holding by 47

sensitive dogs 92

shepherding breeds 45

shouting 21, 29

sit exercises **17**, *32*, 35, 45, 54, 55,
56, *74*, 75, 76, *76*, *78*, *79*, 84, *85*,
86-93, 114, *115*, 130, 132, *132*,
133, *137*, 140, 142, 143,
143, *145*, 153
forward and backward 92-3, **92**
hand signal **50**
ignore and sit 88, **88-9**
leash and collar style 93, **92-3**
puppy training 32, *32*, *33*
sit/stay 35, 55, 75, 94-9, **94-5**,
96-7, **98-99**, 114, 116-7, **116-7**,
118, **118-9**, 120, 122
using food 86, **86-7**
using a hook 90-1, **90-1**
using toys 88, **88-9**
socialization of puppies 30, 34, *125*,
126
spaniels 18
stairways, access to 22
stand exercises **17**, 54, 55, **56**, 84,
85, 100-5, *100*, **100-1**, 114
hand signal **50**
problem solving 104-5, **105**
stand/stay 55, 75, 104, **105**, 114
using collar and leash 102, **102**

using hook 104, **104**
using touch and tickle 102, **103**
using toys 102, **103**
using turn and food 100-1, **100-1**
stay exercises *33*, 37, 54, 55, **56**,
84-123, *85*, **120-1**, 132, 133
down/stay 35, 41, *41*, 55, 106,
110, 114, 118, 120, 122, **123**,
152
for puppies 34, *34*, 35
hand signal **50**
sit/stay 35, 55, 75, 94-9, **94-5**,
96-7, **98-9**, 114, 116-7, **116-7**,
118, **118-9**, 120, 122
stand/stay 55, 75, 104, 114
stroking *21*, 23, 26, 27, *27*, 29, 88,
90, *92*, *133*, *141*, *145*

T

terriers 18, 45

territory 23

tidbits 25, *27*, 33, *33*, 38, 42, 62,
63, *63*, *72*, 75, 79, 80, *81*, 84, *86*,
87, *91*, 93, 95, 101, *101*, *102*,
104, *104*, 106, *107*, *108*, *109*,
115, *119*, 135, *137*, 140, *141*,
144, *145*, *147*, 148, 151; *see also*
treats

timing 47, 49

toilet training 37

toy breeds 21, 42, 45, 83

toys as training aids 10, **16-17**, 25,
25, 32, *32*, 33, *33*, 40, *41*, 46, 56,
62, *63*, 68, *68*, 74, *74*, 75, *75*, 79,
88, **88-9**, 90, 102, **102-3**, *105*,
106, **106-7**, 108, *108*, 109, 120,
121, 127, *127*, 128-131, **128-9**,

130-1, 142, 144, 148, 154; *see
also* food toys
types of 40
training aids **16-17**; *see also* food,
praise, treats, tidbits, toys as
training aids
treats 9, 25; *see also* tidbits
as training aids 10, 41, 70, 71, *71*,
74, *86*, *87*, 90, *90*, *91*, 93, *93*,
104, *104*, 106, *107*, 135, 138,
139, 143, 146, *147*
troubleshooting 154-5

U

unrewarding experiences 45, 46-7

V

visitors 8, 28, 29, 112

vitamin supplements 42

voice commands 35, *48*, 60, *61*, 62,
63, 64, 68, 71, 72, 74, 76, 78, 84,
86, 88, 96, 100, 102, 116, *119*,
155; *see also individual command
words*

voice, use of 46, 49, 59, 60, *61*, 64,
68, 100, 106, 122, *133*

W-X-Y-Z

walks 26, 113, *113*, 114, 130, 152,
155
with a stroller 78-9, *79*

water pistols 31

whistles 35, 42, *43*, 50, 56, 134-7,
134, *137*, 144, **144-5**, 146, **146-
7**, 148, *148*, *149*

wolves 8, 20, 24, 44, 49, 126, 148

Acknowledgments

Author's Acknowledgments

There are several people whom I would like to thank for their help in the preparation of this book. A big vote of appreciation to:

Ross McCarthy for his immense help and skills as a trainer and behavior practitioner.

All the clients and friends who allowed us to photograph themselves and their dogs for the book. Specifically thanks to Spencer Boyle, Christine Brannan, Anne Brierly, Maggie Buckle, Judy Cooper, Margaret Cornwell, Julie Forward, Mike Johnson, Simone Le Boff, Sue McCarthy, Caroline McKernan, Tracey Neal, Diane Peters, Les Read, Tracey Thompkins, Angie Towse and Chrissie Yggmark.

Mrs. M. J. Litton for setting me on the road to success in the world of dogs.

Judy Cooper for training assistance.

All my dogs.

Finally I would like to thank Malcolm, Neil, Philip and Kevin, who helped me turn this idea for a book into reality.

Colin Tennant, 2004

Picture Credits

Unless otherwise credited below, all the photographs in this book were taken by Neil Sutherland in studios established on location in Hertfordshire or in his home studio in Billingshurst, West Sussex.

RSPCA: 30 (Cheryl A. Ertelt), 31 (A. E. Janes).

Colin Tennant for Interpet: 25 lower right; 37 lower right; 61 lower left; 79 lower.

Further Information

Readers seeking more advice and information about a broad range of topics concerning dog training and behavior are invited to visit Colin Tennant's website (www.colintennant.co.uk).